BOOK • VIDEO

SCOTTY ANDERSON
RED HOT GUITAR

CONTENTS

Biography 2
Selected Discography..................................... 3
Chapter 1: Double Stops................................ 4
Chapter 2: Chord Voicings............................ 6
Chapter 3: Single-Note Lines 9
Chapter 4: String Bending and Sequences 14
Chapter 5: Open-Voiced Double Stops 16
Chapter 6: Double-Stop Runs 22
Chapter 7: Fingerstyle Technique 26
Chapter 8: Scales, Licks, Runs and Rhythms 30
Chapter 9: Chord-Based Double Stops and Riffs 33
Chapter 10: Chet Atkins-Style Performance 42
Chapter 11: Chord Melody 51
Chapter 12: Advanced Harmonization 55
Chapter 13: Harp Harmonics 61
Chapter 14: Three-Note Chord Riffs and Licks in A... 66
Chapter 15: Melodic Fingerstyle 72
Guitar Notation Legend 76

To access video visit:
www.halleonard.com/mylibrary
Enter Code
4584-2252-7745-4743

ISBN: 978-1-5400-6553-7

Copyright © 1991, 2006, 2022 Hot Licks Productions, Inc.
All Rights Reserved   Used by Permission

No part of this publication may be reproduced in any form or by
any means without the prior written permission of the Publisher.

Visit Hal Leonard Online at
www.halleonard.com

Contact us:
Hal Leonard
7777 West Bluemound Road
Milwaukee, WI 53213
Email: info@halleonard.com

In Europe, contact:
Hal Leonard Europe Limited
42 Wigmore Street
Marylebone, London, W1U 2RN
Email: info@halleonardeurope.com

In Australia, contact:
Hal Leonard Australia Pty. Ltd.
4 Lentara Court
Cheltenham, Victoria, 3192 Australia
Email: info@halleonard.com.au

BIOGRAPHY

Guitarist Scotty Anderson was born in 1954, in Cincinnati, Ohio, into a very musical family. His father, Herschel "Boog" Anderson, played guitar and fiddle; his mother played guitar; and his father's young brother, Dillard Anderson, was a guitarist and pedal steel player.

By age 19, Anderson was practiced at guitar playing and began creating a name for himself around the local roadhouses both in his hometown and in the northern Kentucky region.

Around this time, Anderson discovered the early work of guitarist Chet Atkins, whose diverse playing and unique technical skills had Anderson hooked immediately. As he got older and more experienced, Anderson dedicated himself to teaching, offering local workshops and seminars.

He also took the stage at several shows during this time, though it wasn't until the 1990s that Anderson committed to touring and playing on the national rockabilly scene.

In 2000, *Guitar One* magazine named Anderson one of the top 10 unknown guitarists in the U.S.

During his tenure as a professional musician, Anderson has released three solo albums, all of which demonstrate his diverse tastes and Atkins-like technical prowess.

His solo debut, *Sleight of Hand*, was released on the regional label Magnum Records, in 1985, and featured Anderson's interpretations of jazz and rockabilly classics ranging from "On Green Dolphin Street" to "Mystery Train."

In 2001, Anderson released *Triple Stop* on the blues and roots label J Curve Records. The instrumental album centers on Anderson's virtuoso-level guitar playing, covering styles from bebop and boogie to straight-ahead and country. That same year, the guitarist won the Cincinnati Area Music award (CAMMY) for best jazz instrumentalist.

Anderson's 2003 disc, *Classic Scotty* (J Curve) showcased his love of blending gritty blues and sophisticated jazz.

Since that time, Anderson has continued to play regularly in the greater Cincinnati area, in addition to maintaining a busy teaching schedule.

SELECT DISCOGRAPHY

Sleight of Hand (Magnum Records, 1985)

Triple Stop (J Curve Records, 2001)

Classic Scotty (J Curve Records, 2003)

SUGGESTED LISTENING

Chet Atkins *Essential* (RCA, 1996)

George Benson *In Your Eyes* (Warner Bros/WEA, 1990)

Eddie Cochran *Somethin' Else: The Fine Lookin' Hits of Eddie Cochran* (Razor & Tie, 1998)

Carl Perkins *Original Sun Greatest Hits* (Rhino/WEA 1987/1990)

Gene Vincent *The Screaming End: The Best of Gene Vincent* (Razor & Tie, 1997)

Compilations *Nashville Guitars* (Lightyear, 2000)
Rockabilly Riot (Sanctuary Records, 2003)

Chapter 1: Double Stops

Example 1
(1:00)

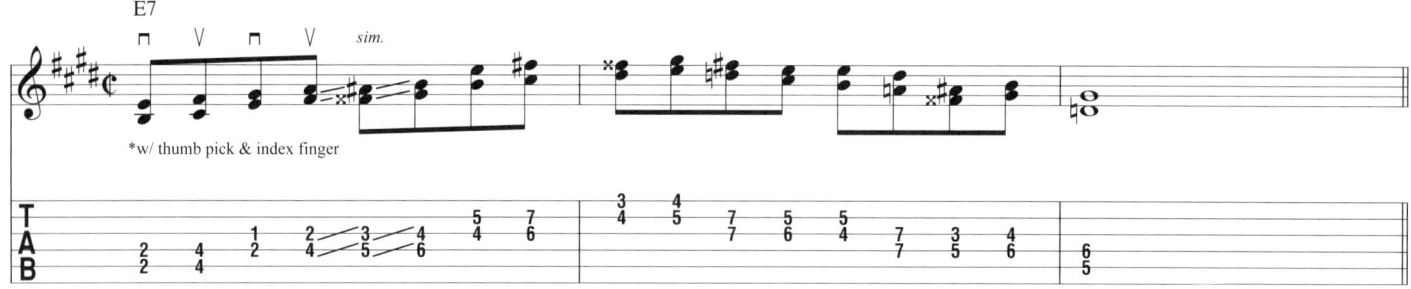

*Double pick w/ thumb & index finger. Hold tightly together & pick as one unit.

Example 2
(1:28)

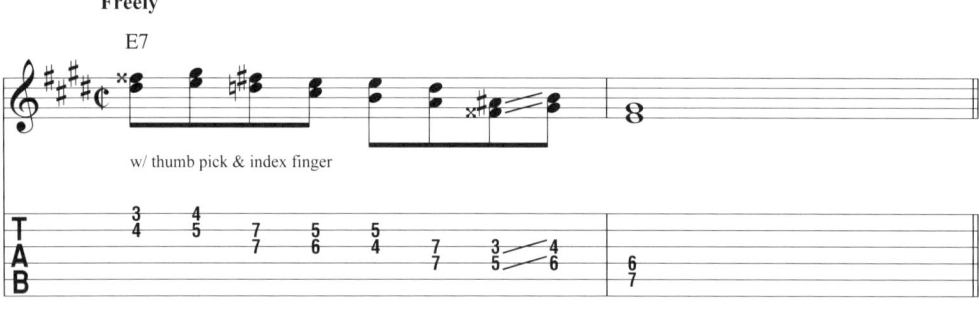

Example 3
(2:36)

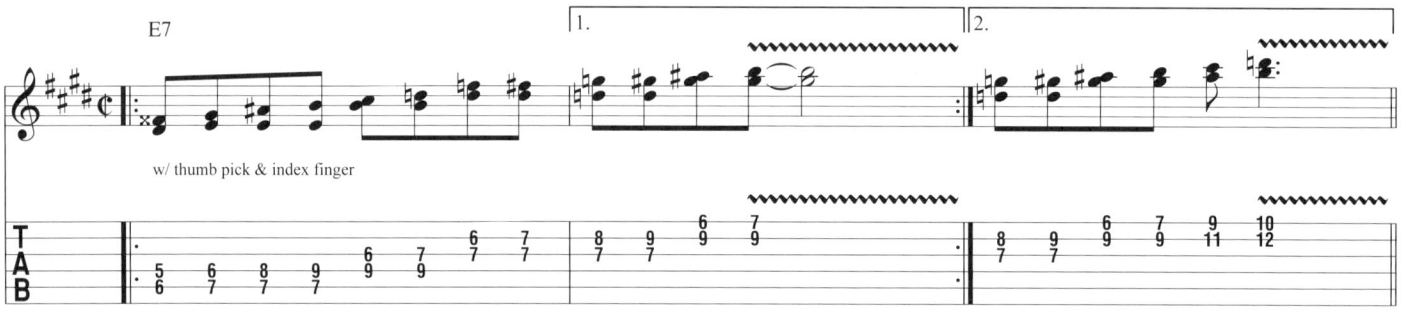

Example 4
(3:05)

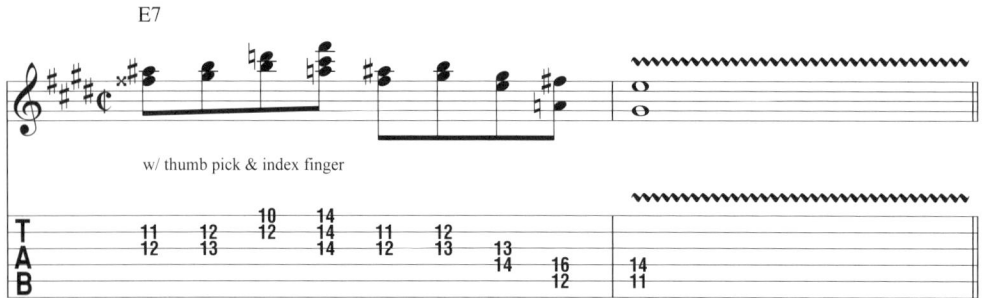

Example 5

(3:29)

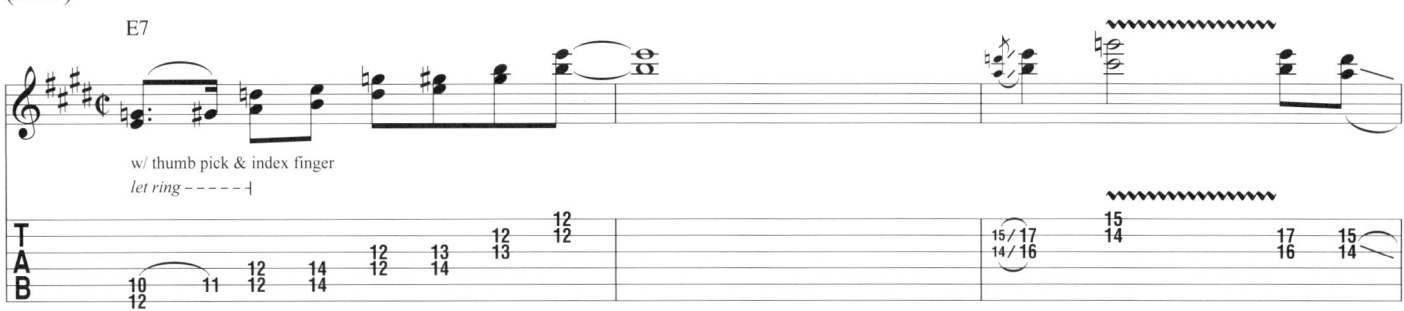

Example 6

(3:45)

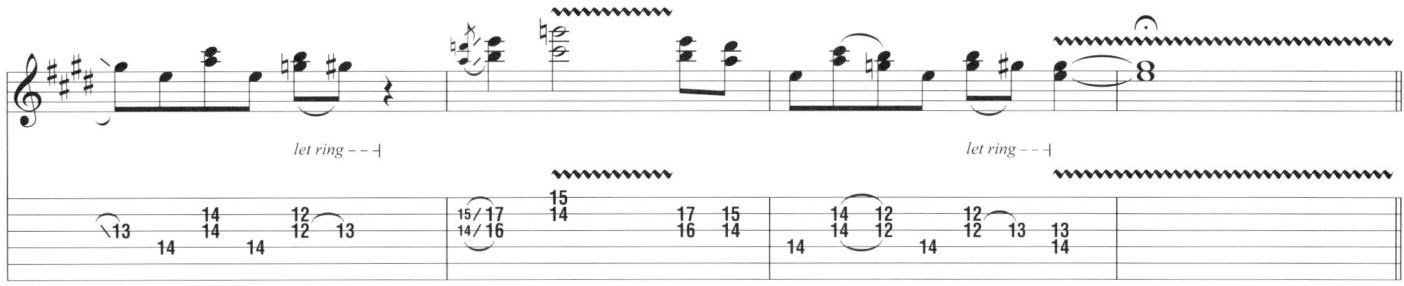

Example 7

(4:14)

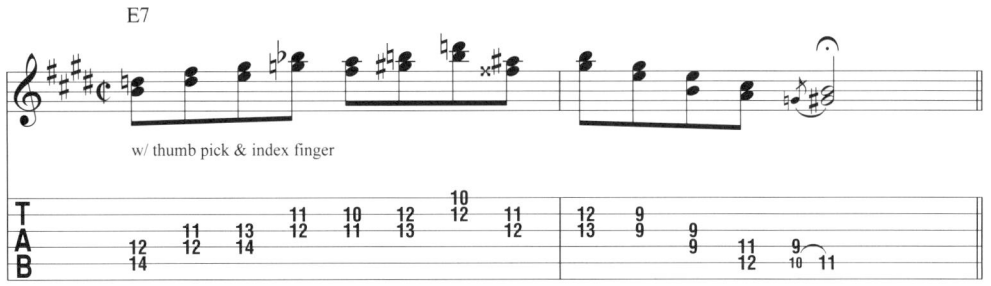

Example 8

(4:44)

Chapter 2: Chord Voicings

Example 9
(:21)

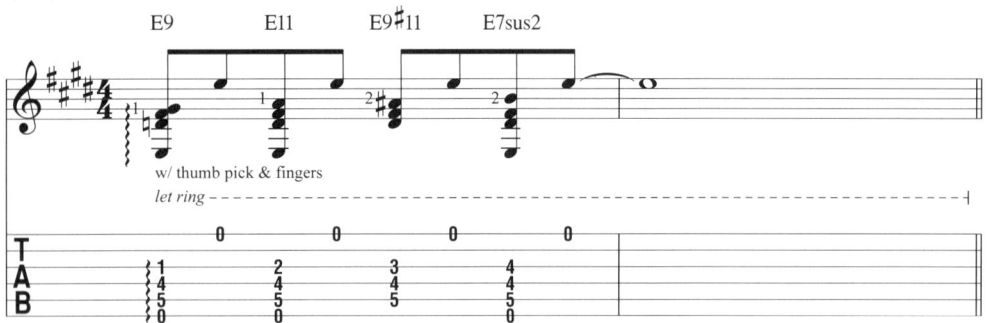

Example 10
(:26)

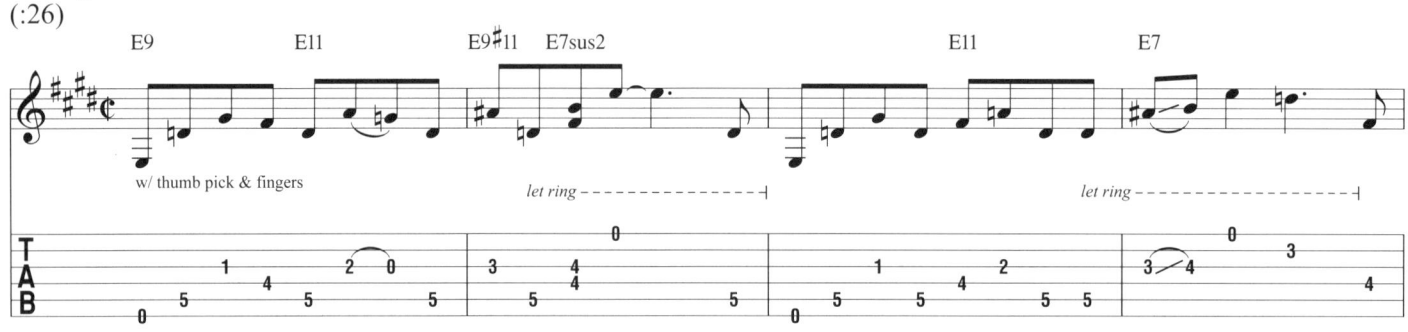

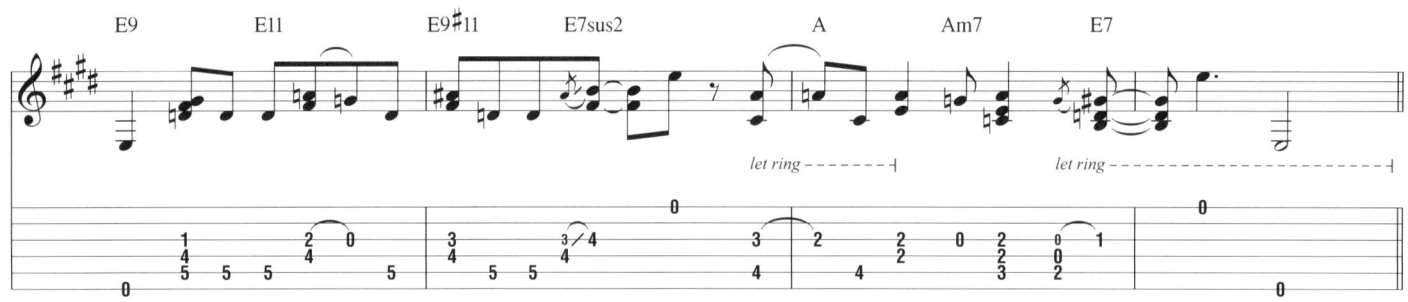

Example 11
(1:43)

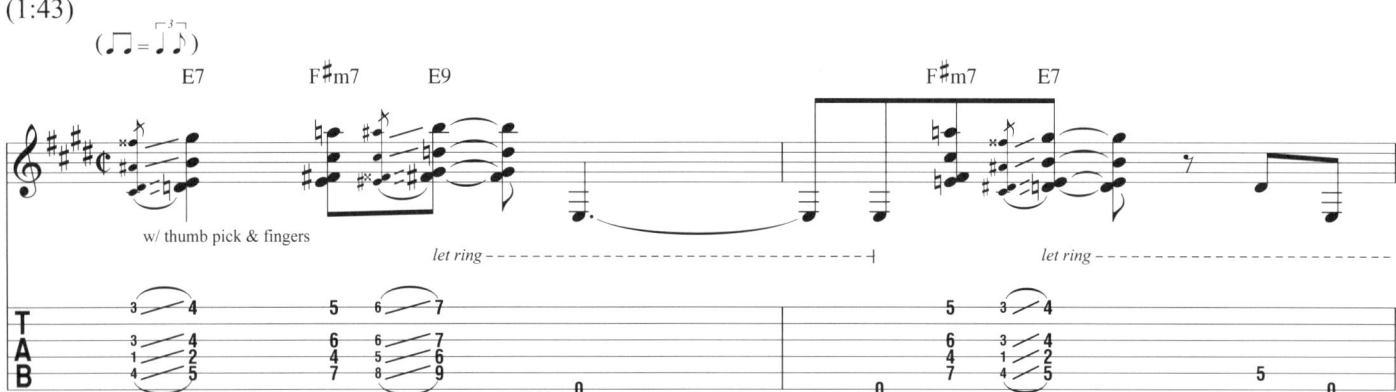

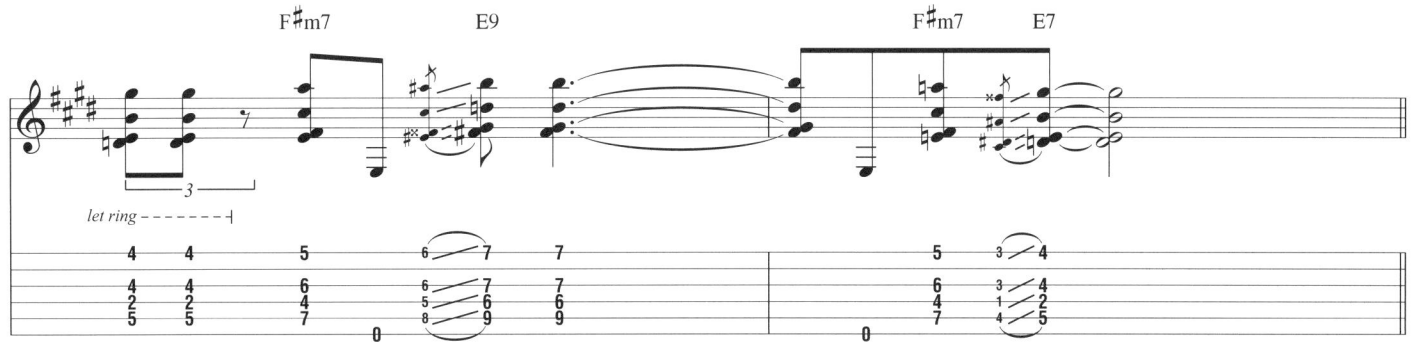

Example 12
(2:07)

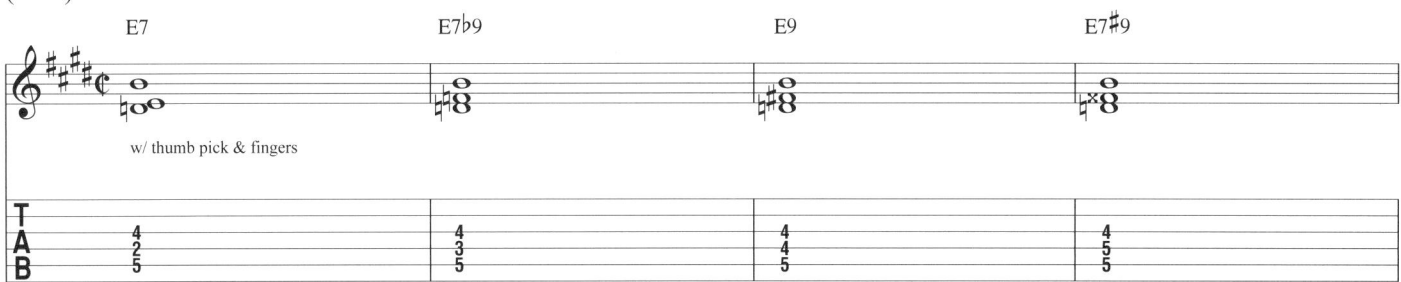

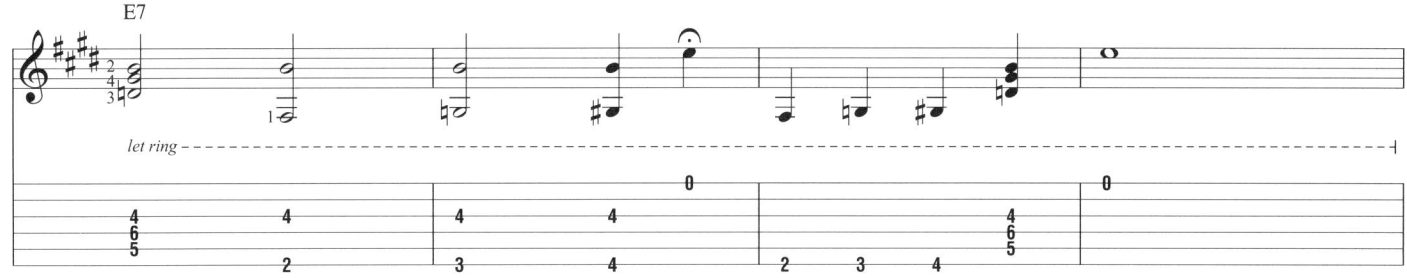

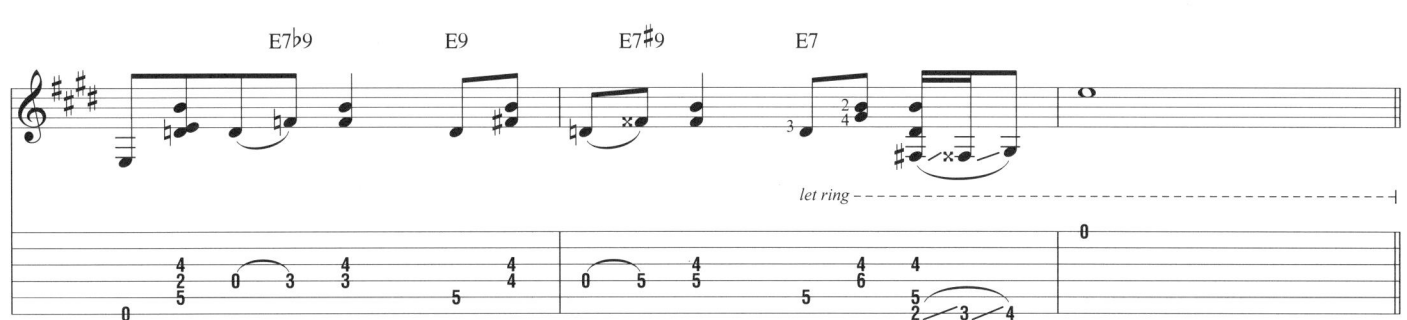

Example 13
(2:28)

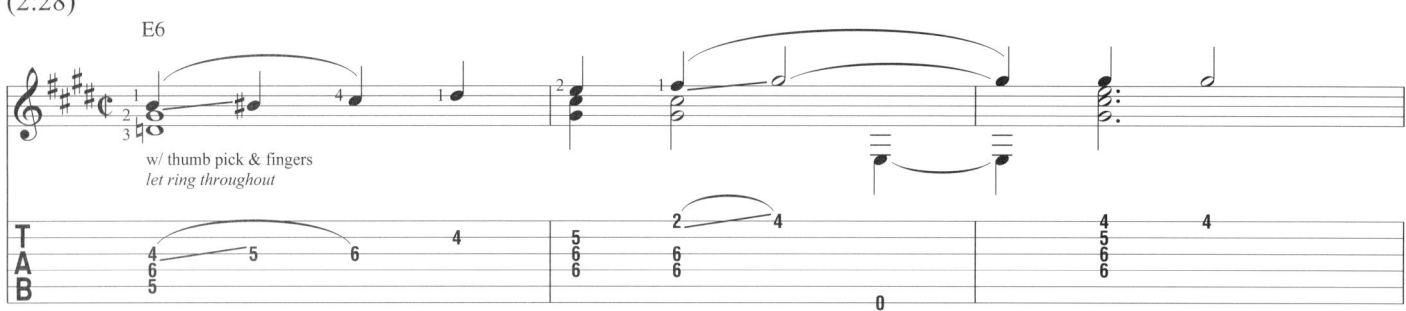

Example 14
(2:45)

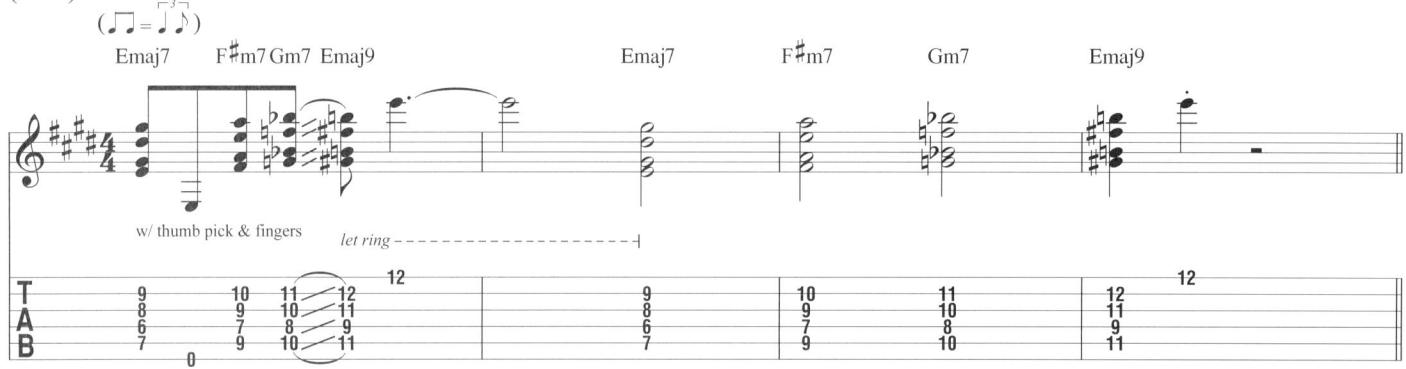

Example 15
(3:14)

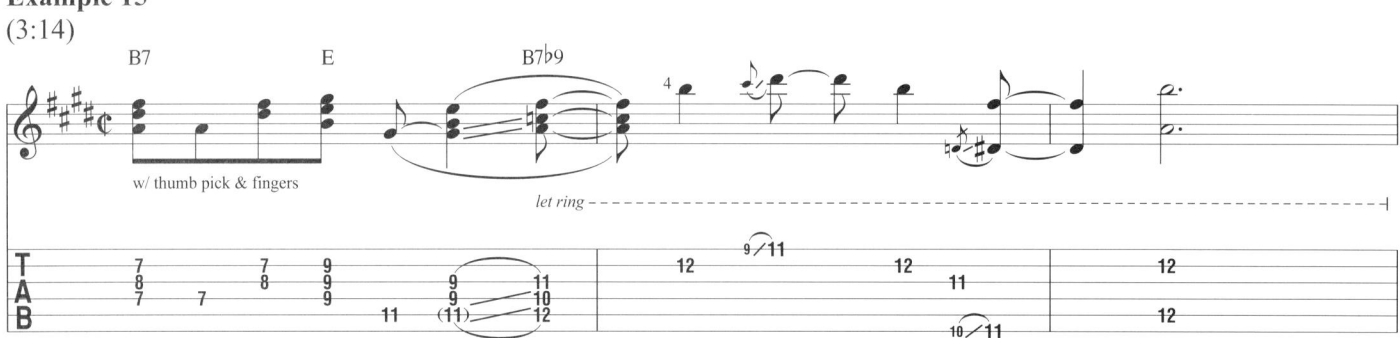

Chapter 3: Single-Note Lines

Example 16
(:11)

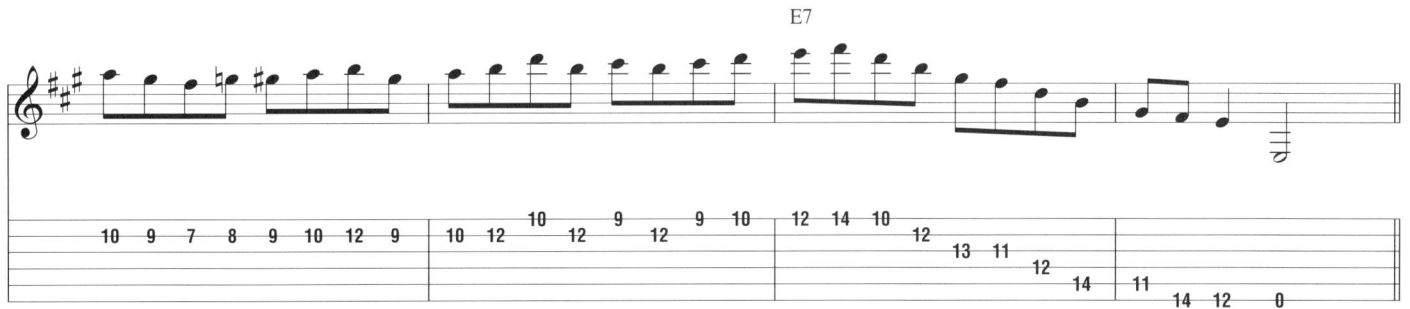

Example 17
(:18)

Example 18
(:26)

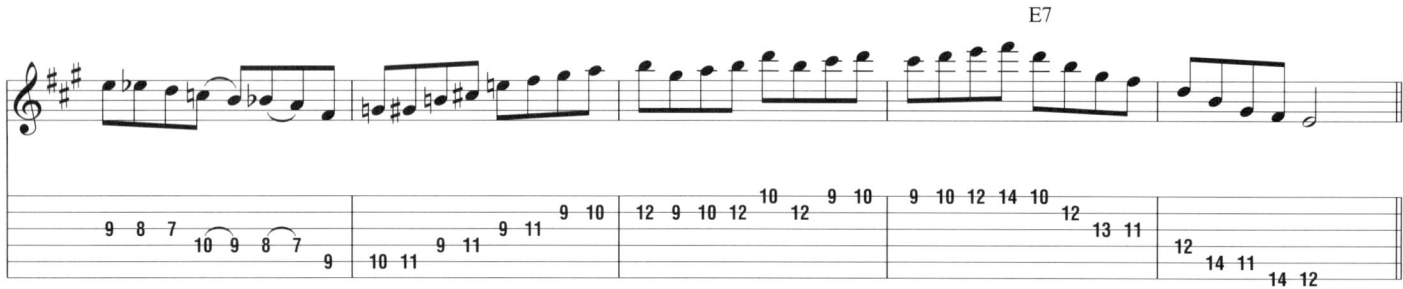

Example 19
(:49)

Example 20
(1:29)

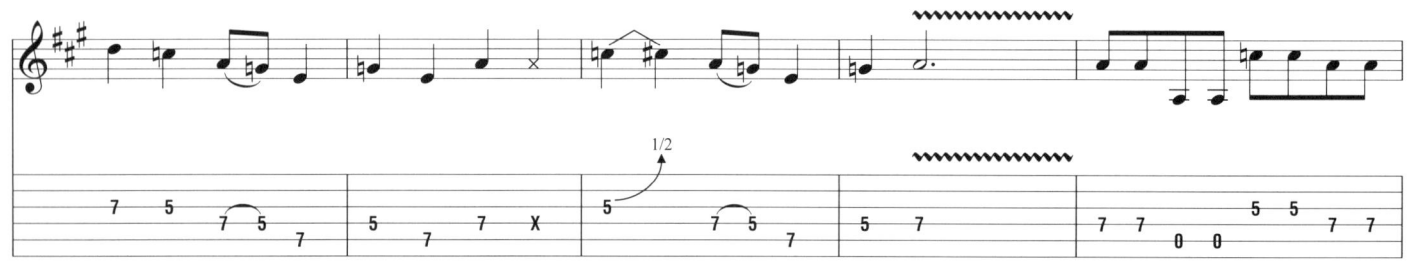

Example 21
(1:43)

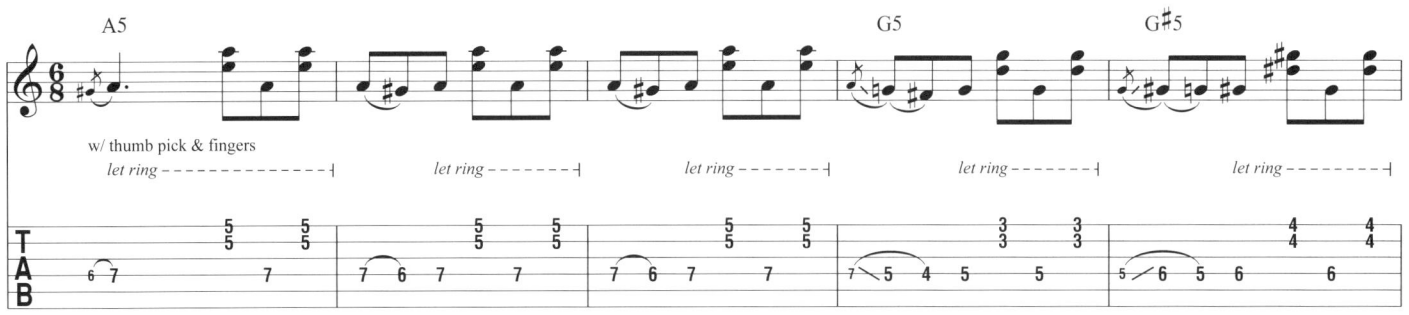

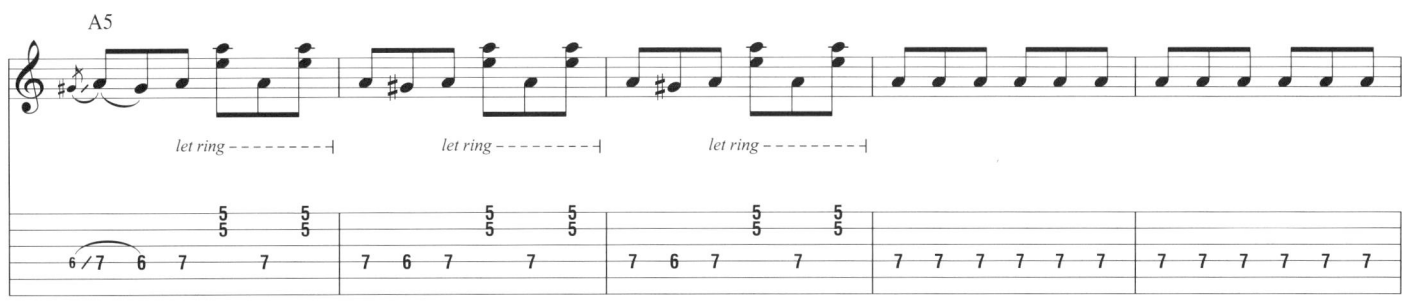

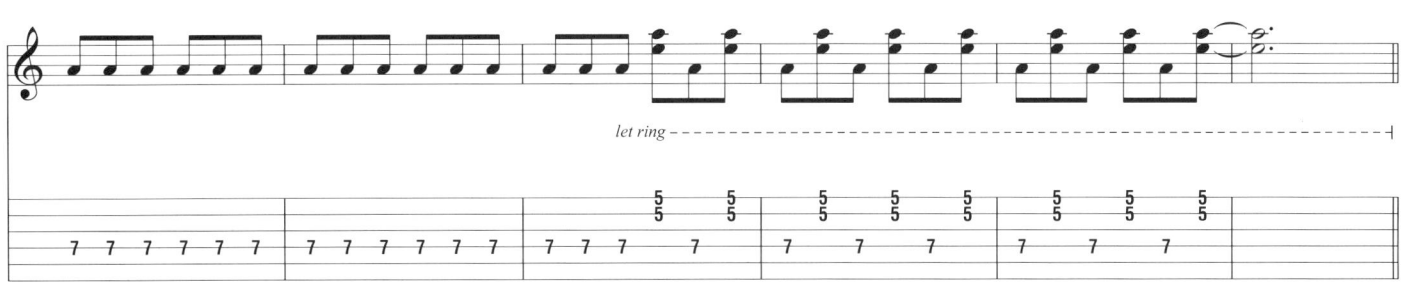

Example 22

(2:01)

*Pick bend notation: p = thumb, i = index, m = middle, a = ring

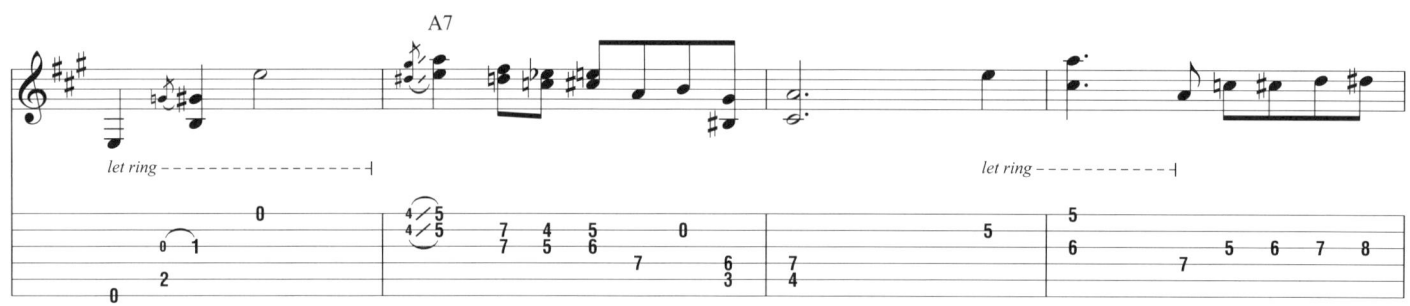

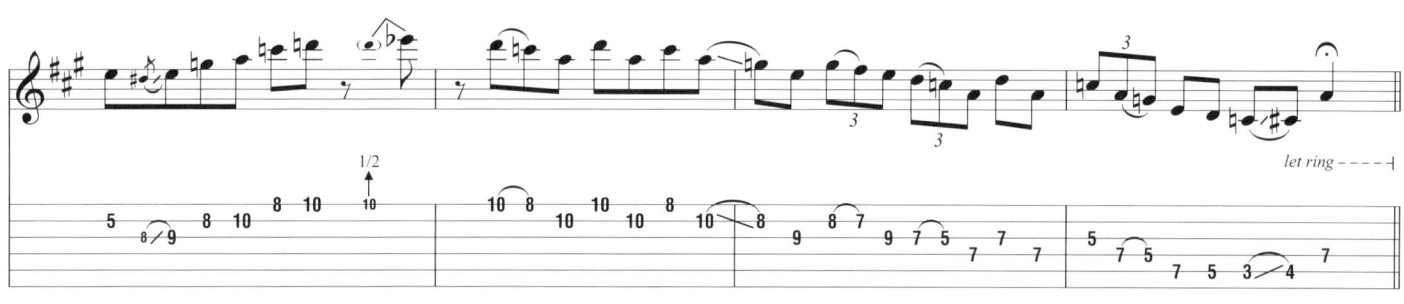

Example 23
(2:14)

*Snap string w/ index finger.

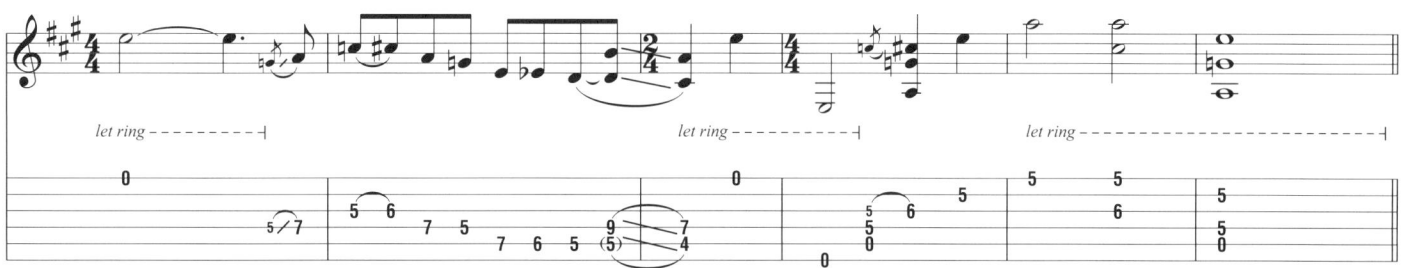

Example 24
(2:33)

13

Chapter 4: String Bending and Sequences

Example 25
(:11)

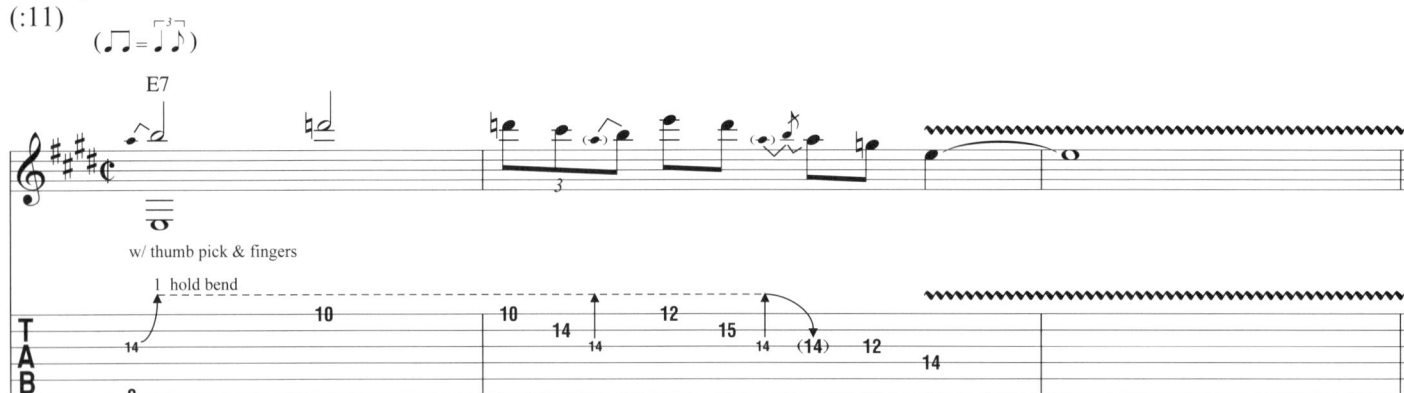

Example 26
(:17)

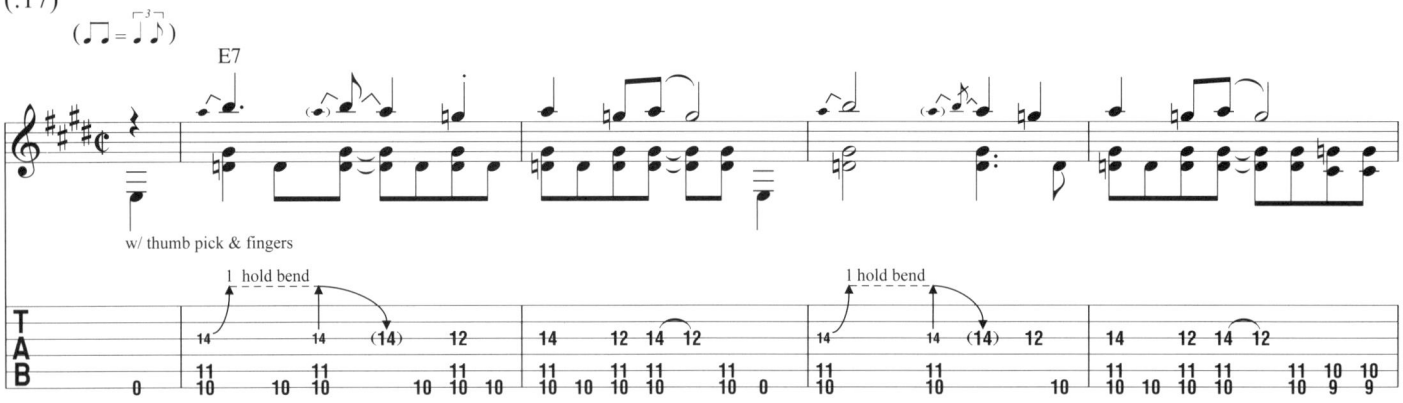

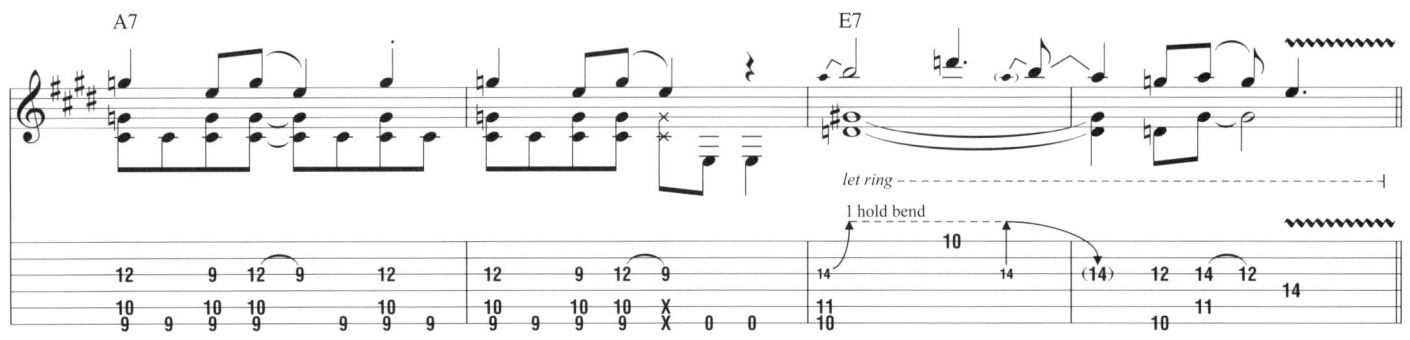

Example 27
(:52)

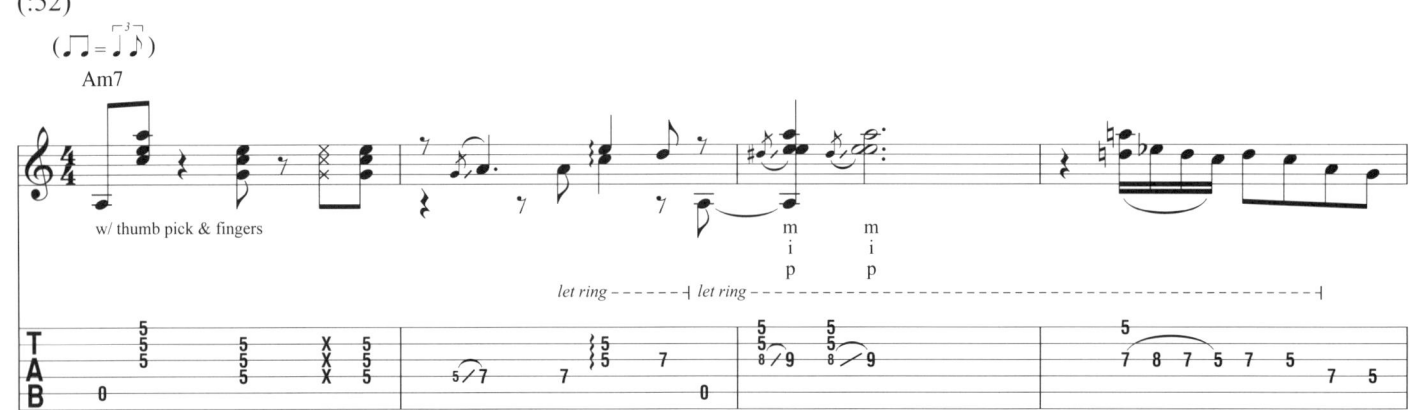

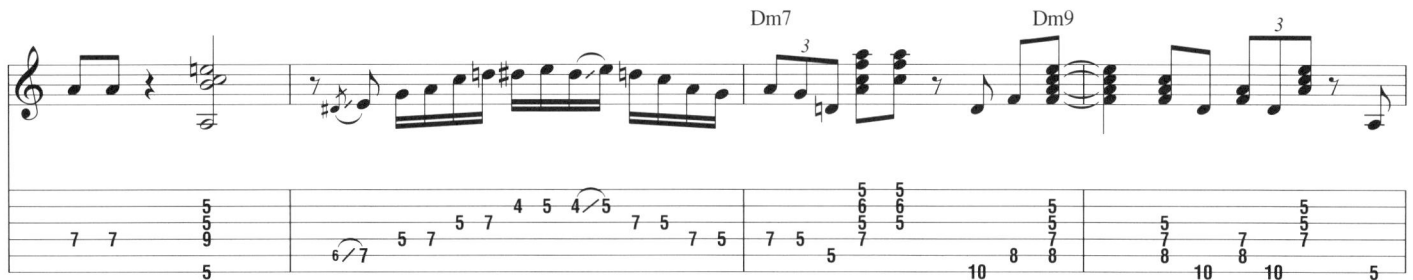

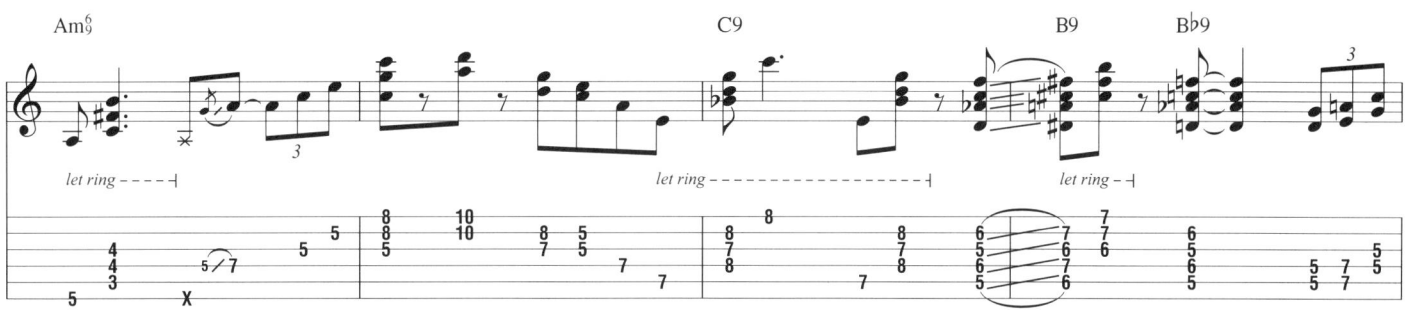

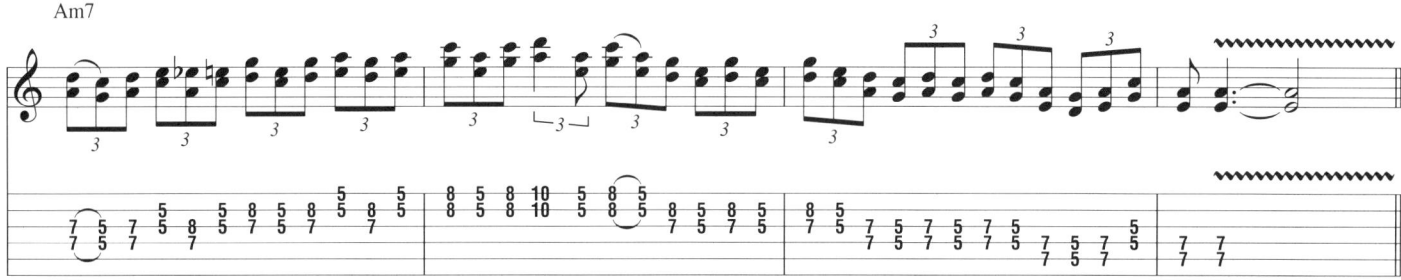

Example 28
(1:34)

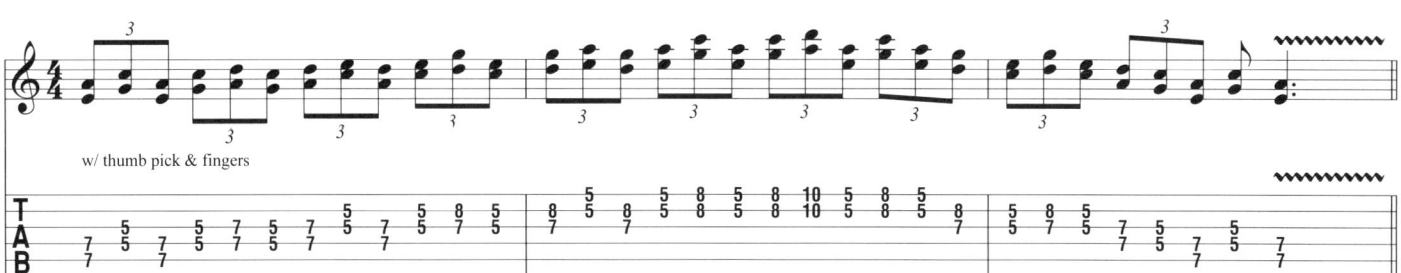

Example 29
(2:01)

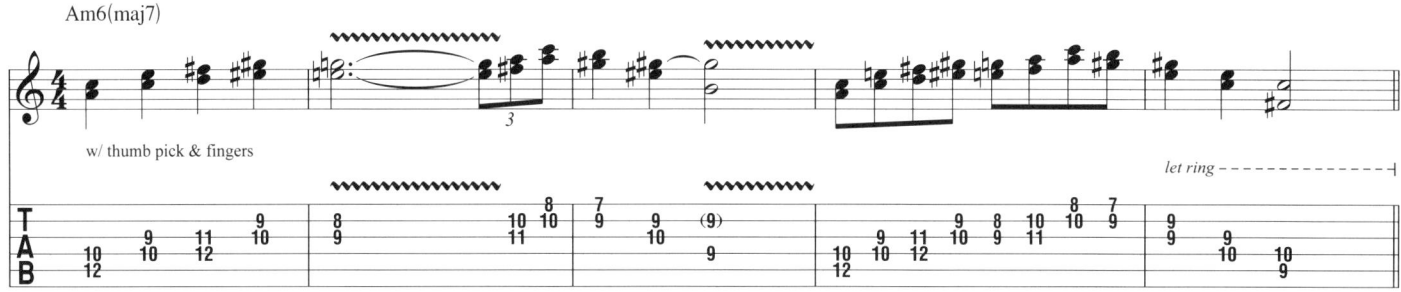

15

Chapter 5: Open-Voiced Double Stops

Example 30
(:01)

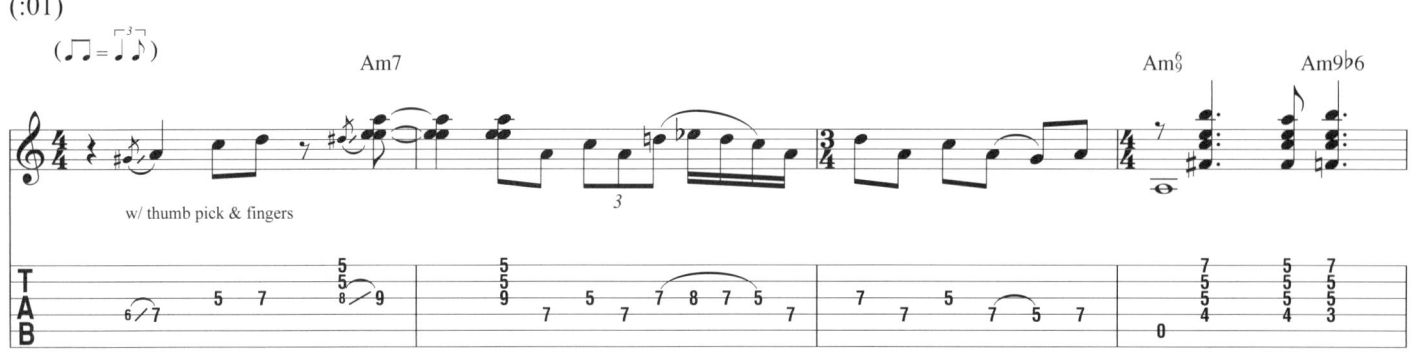

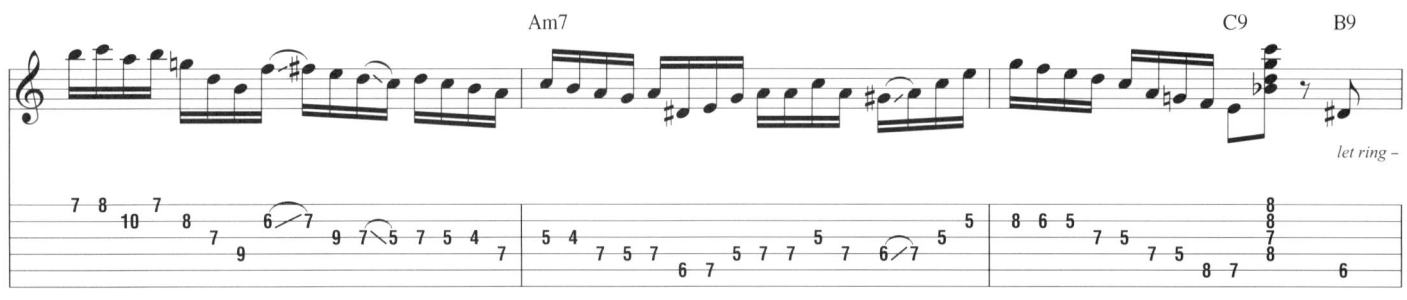

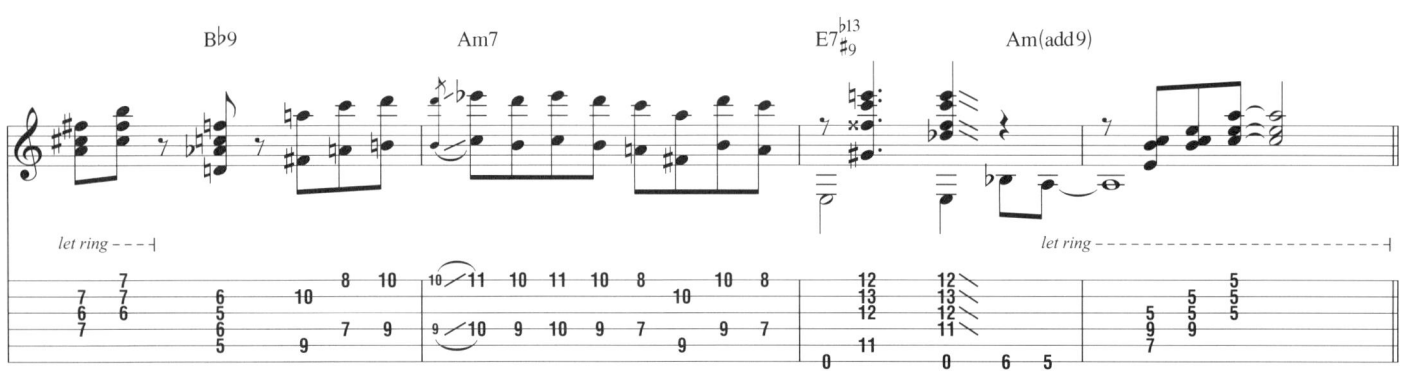

Example 31
(1:07)

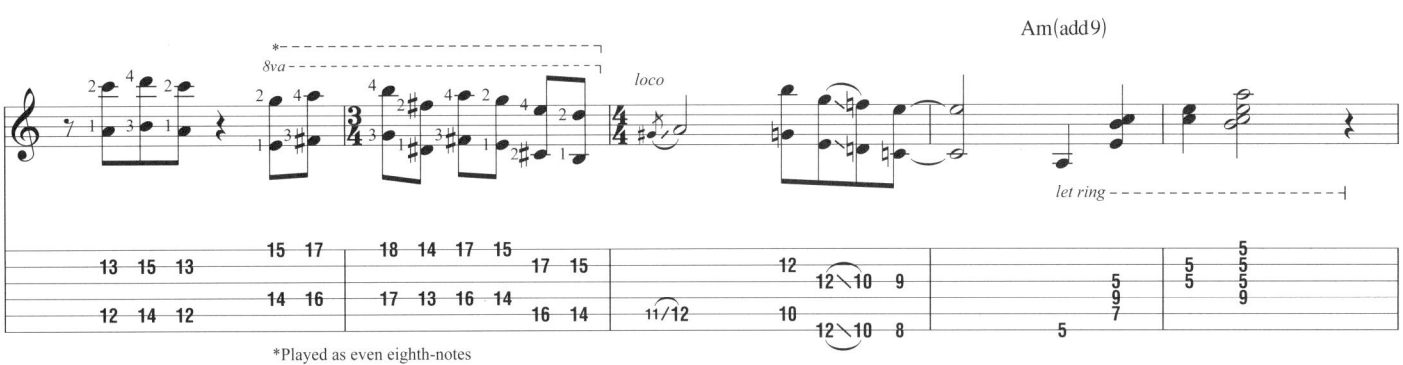

*Played as even eighth-notes

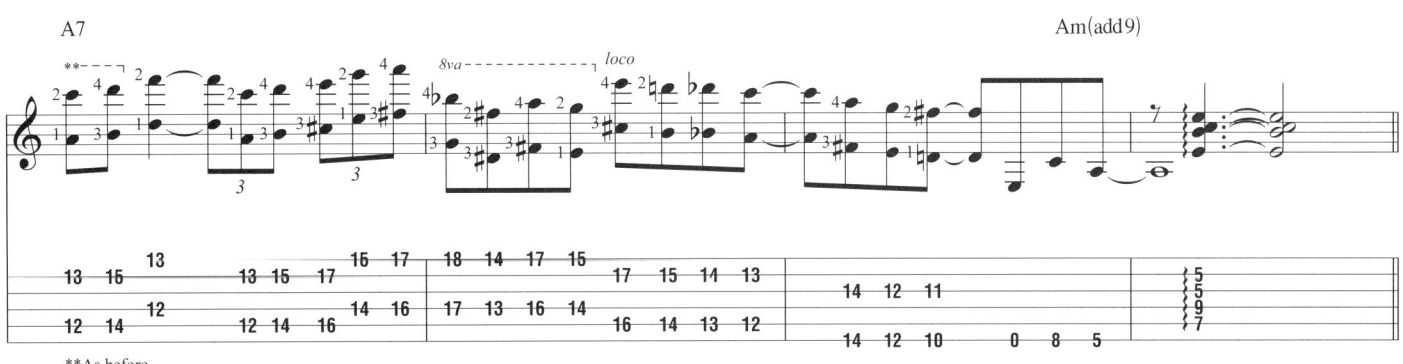

**As before

Example 32
(1:30)

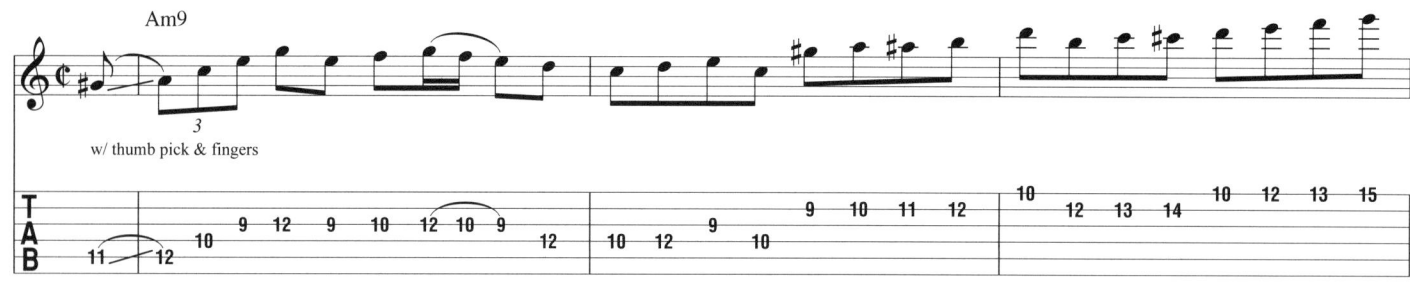

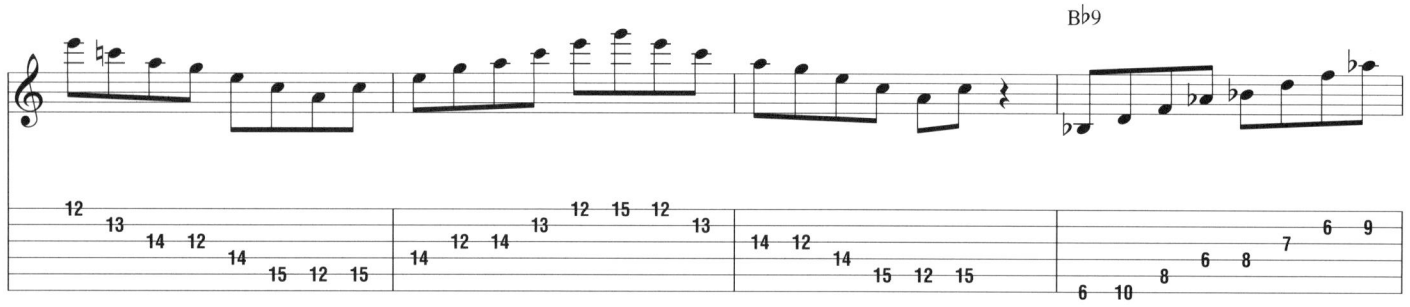

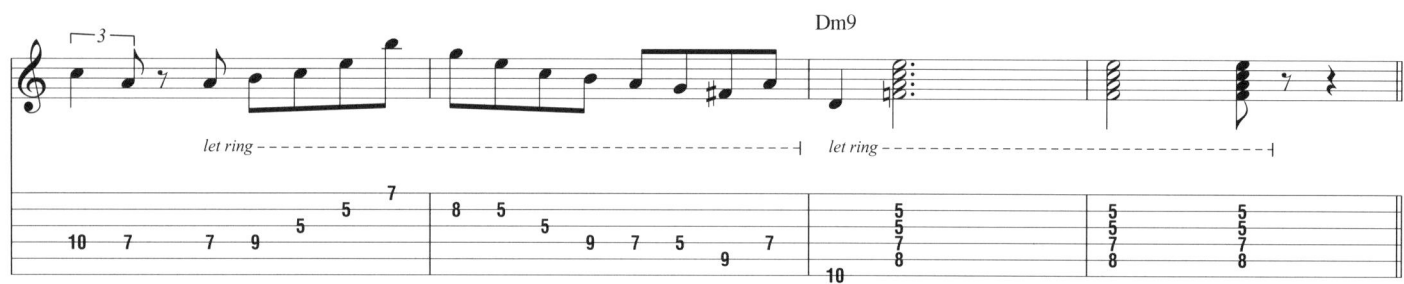

Example 33
(2:28)

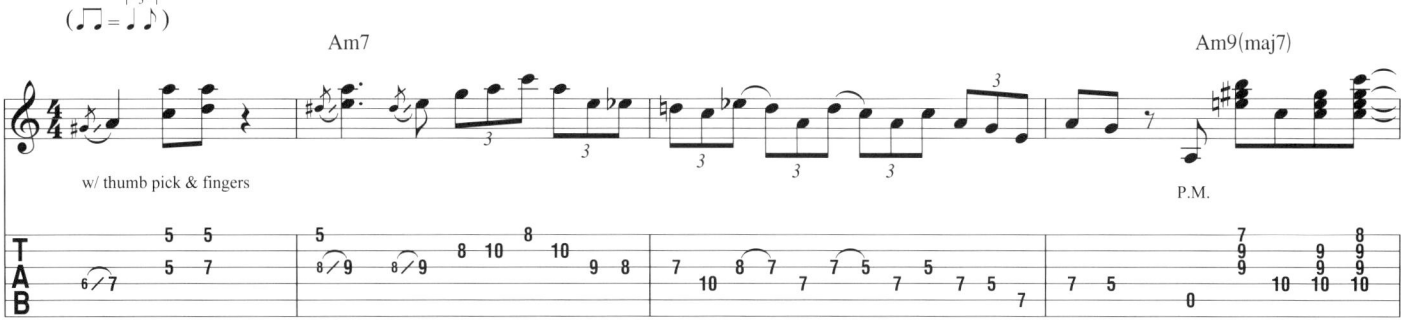
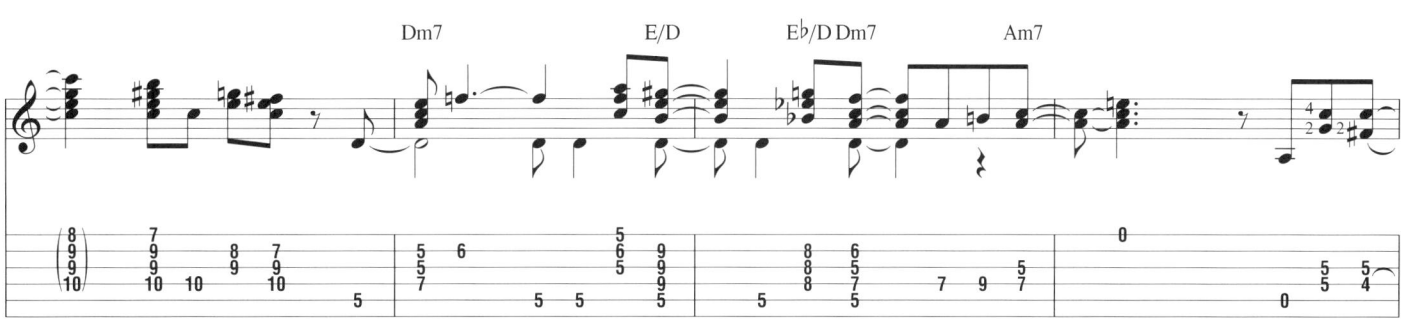
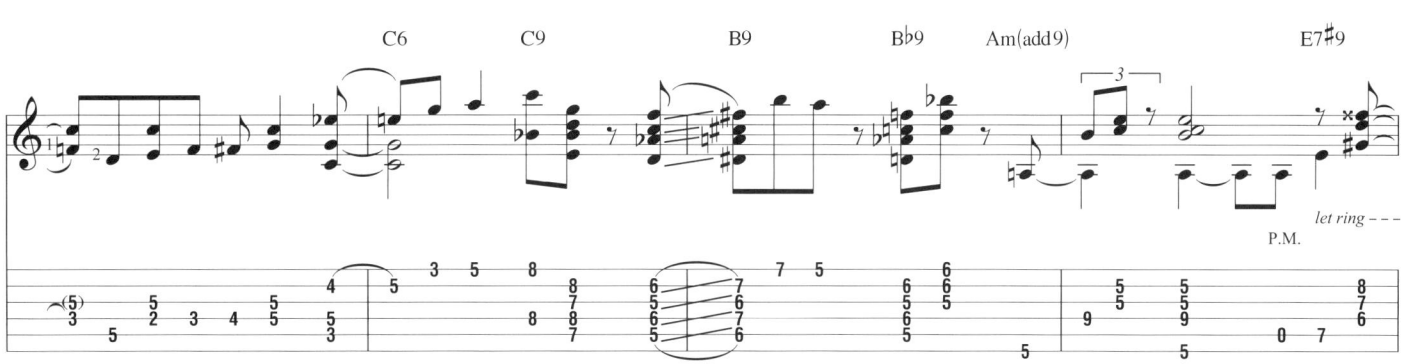

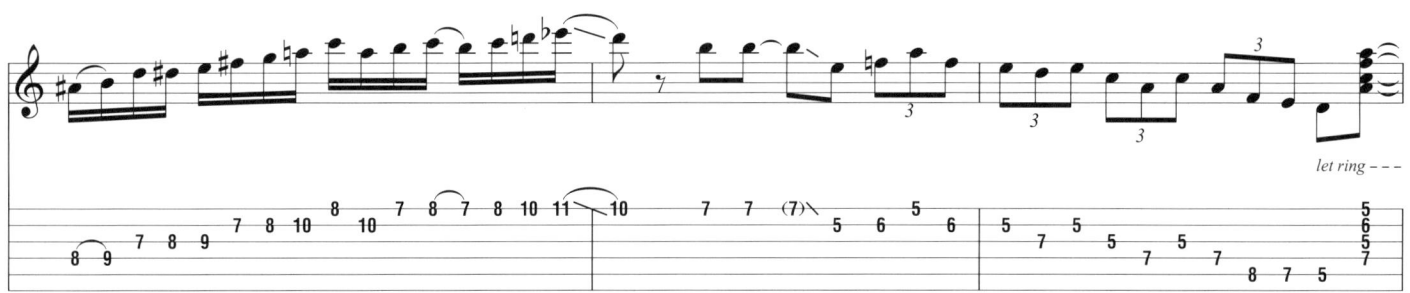

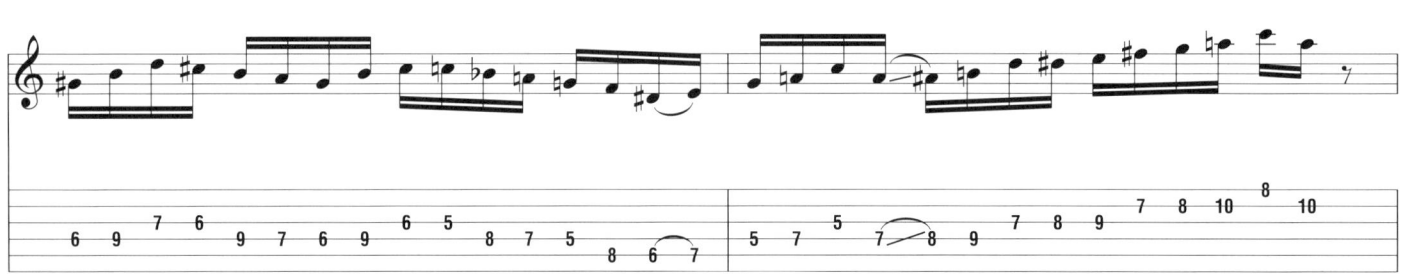

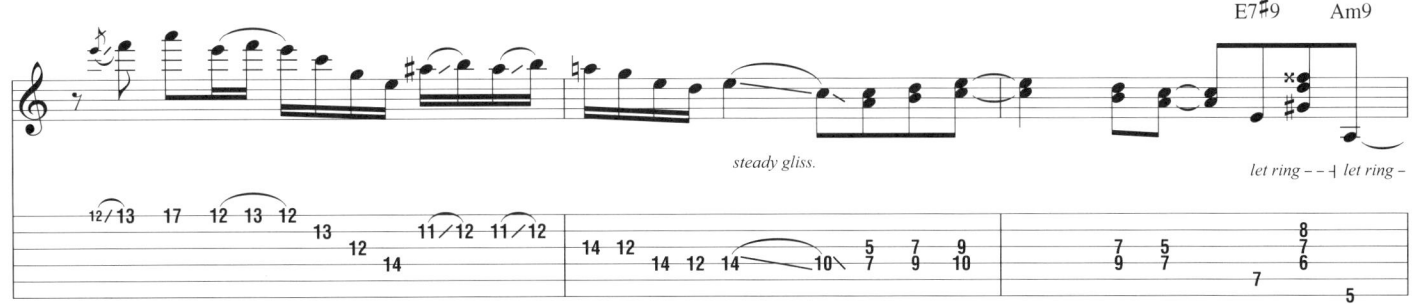
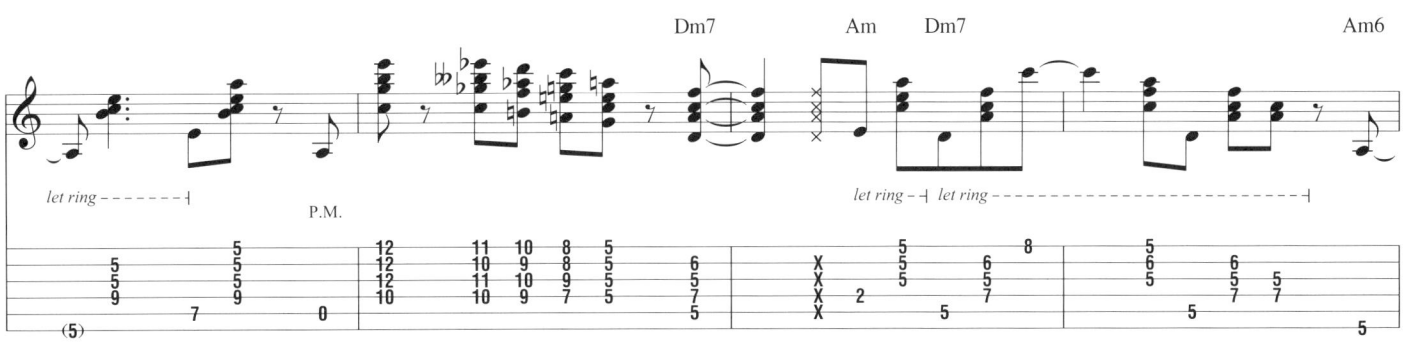

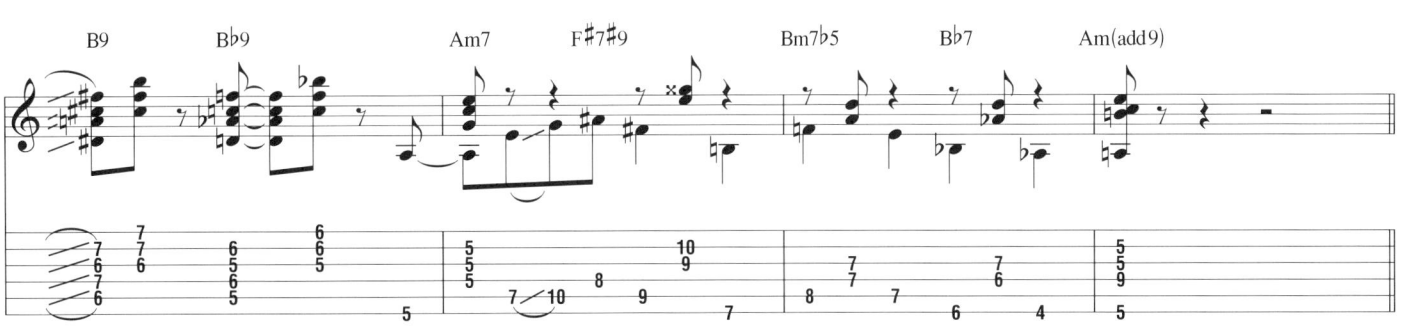

21

Chapter 6: Double-Stop Runs

Example 34
(:17)

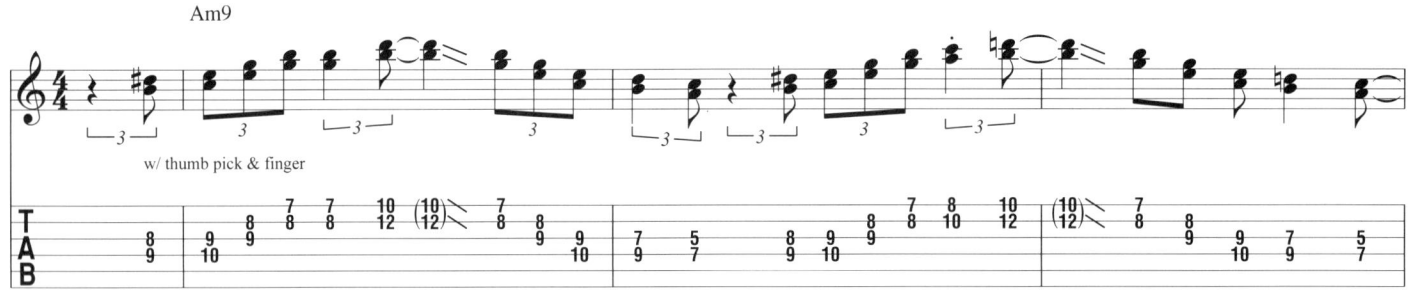

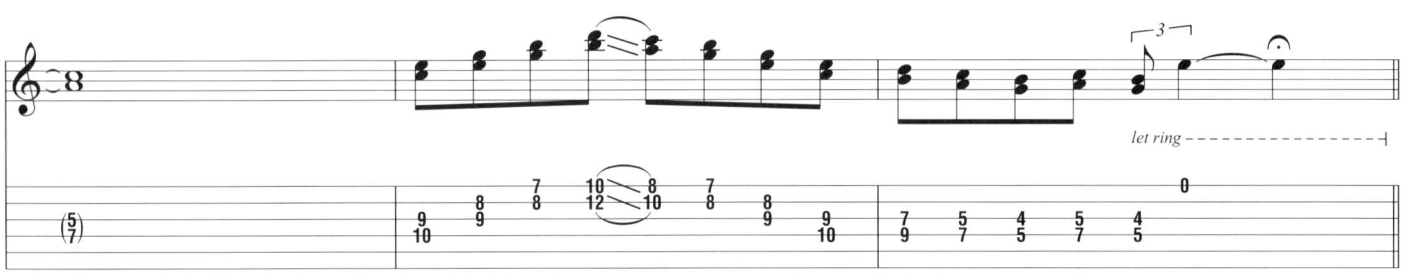

Example 35
(:36)

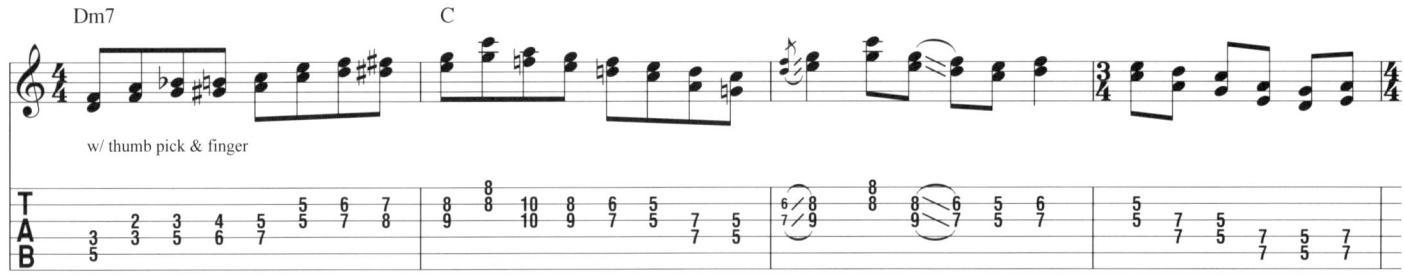

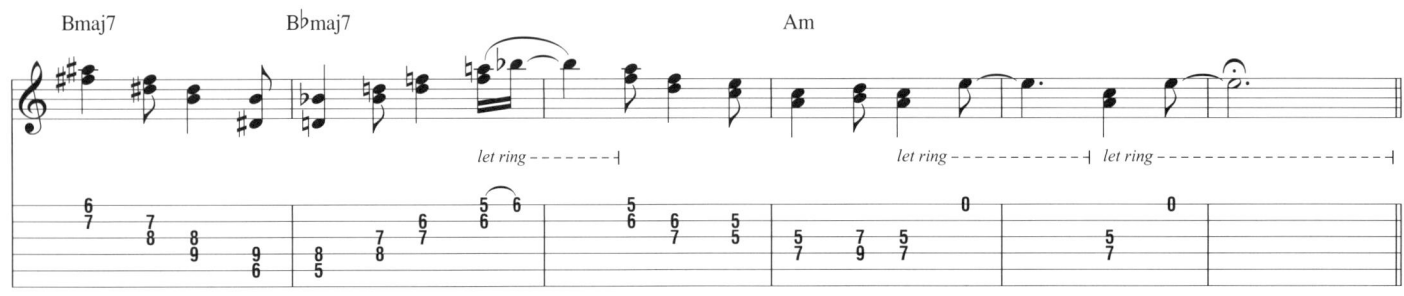

Example 36

(:49)

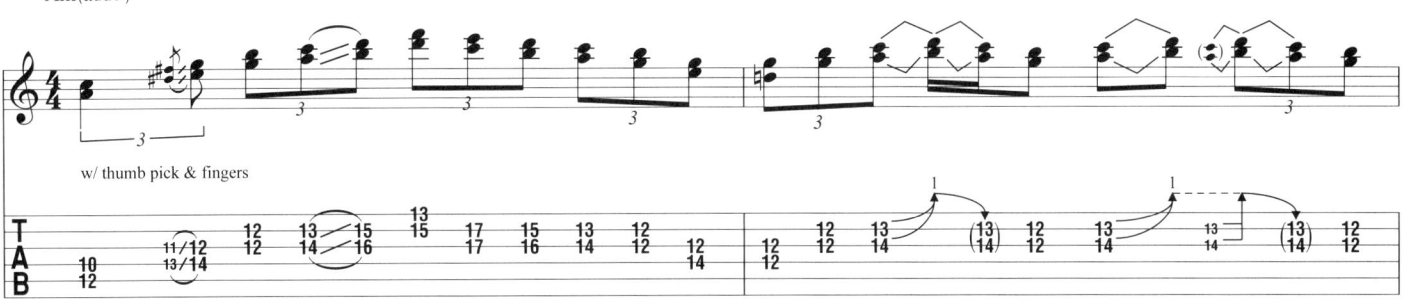

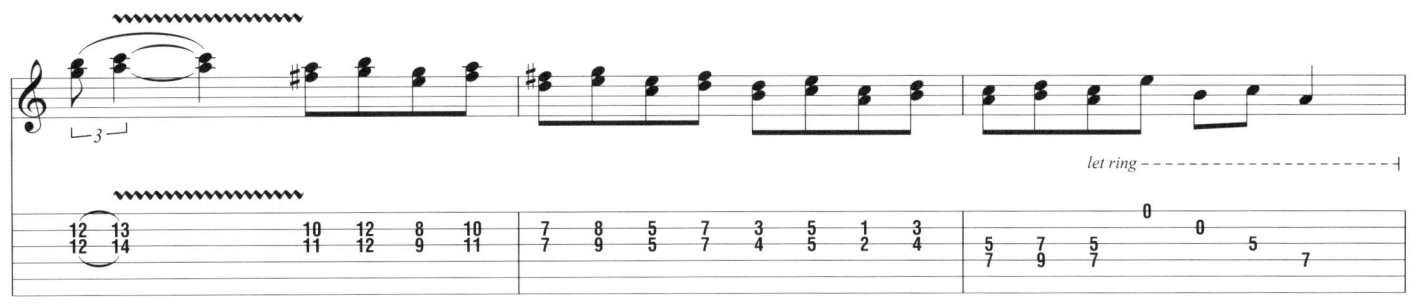

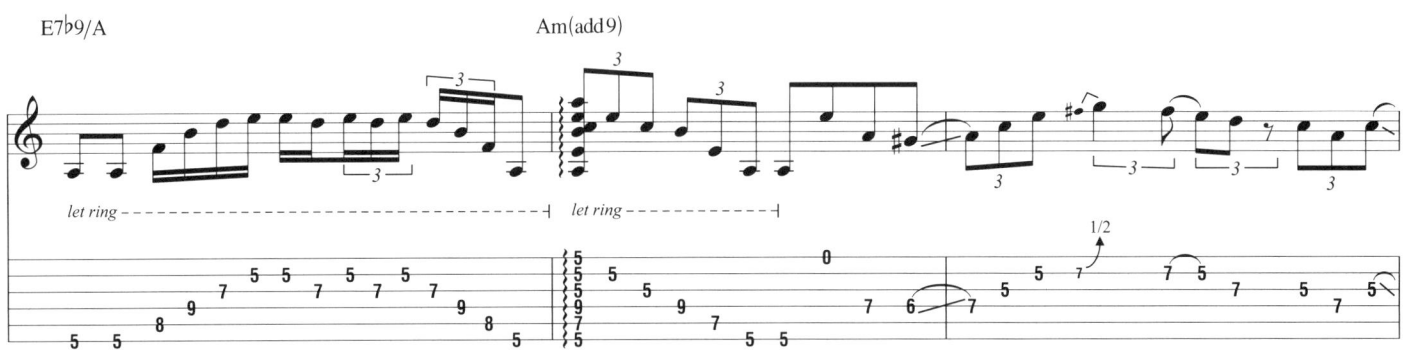

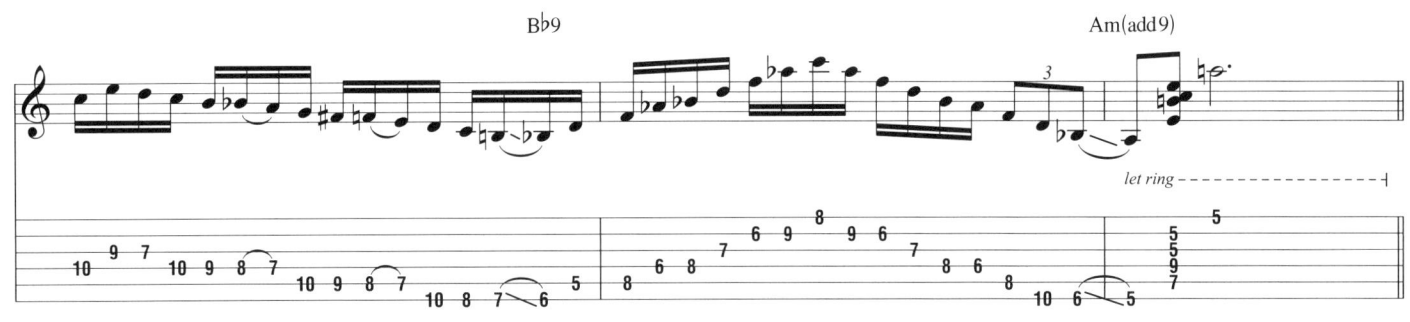

Example 37
(1:11)

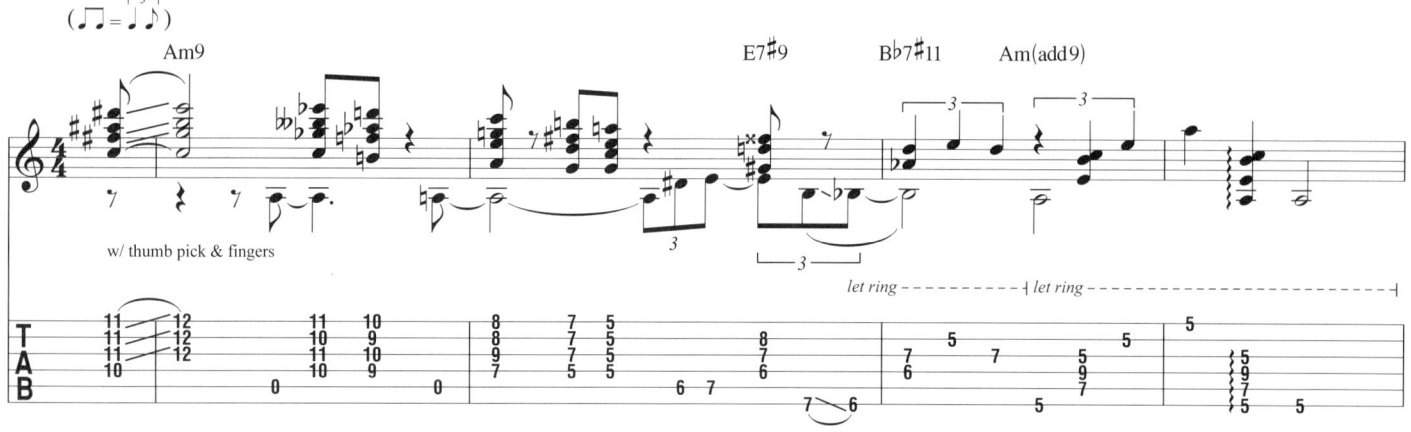

Example 38
(1:34)

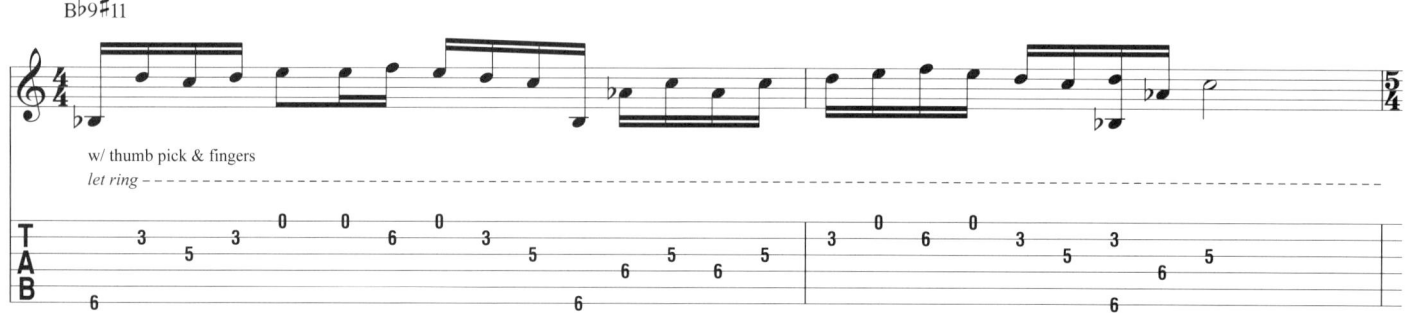

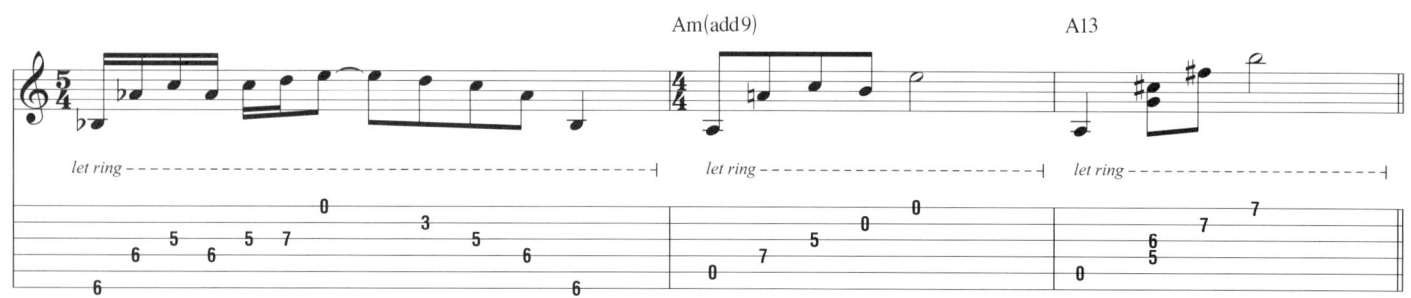

Example 39
(1:52)

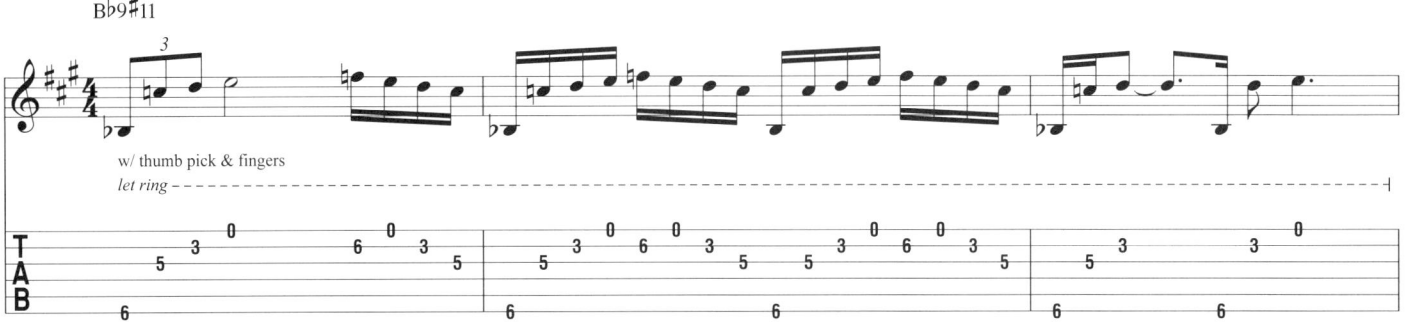

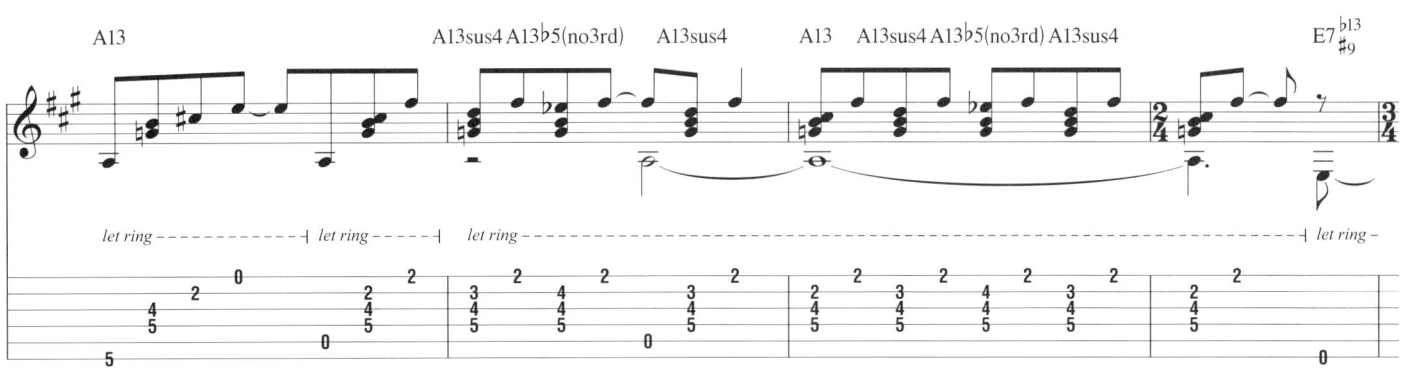

*T = Thumb on 6th string

Chapter 7: Fingerstyle Technique

Example 40
(:06)

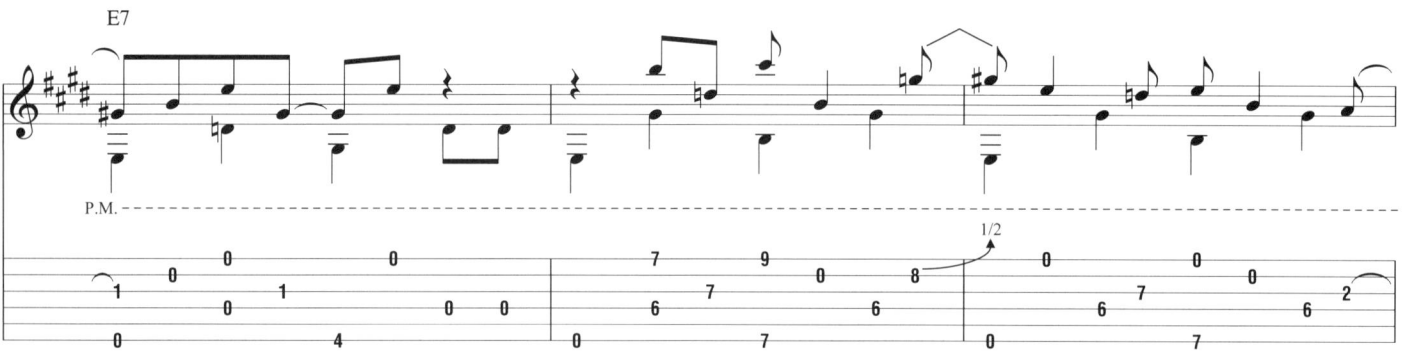

*Down stemmed notes only.

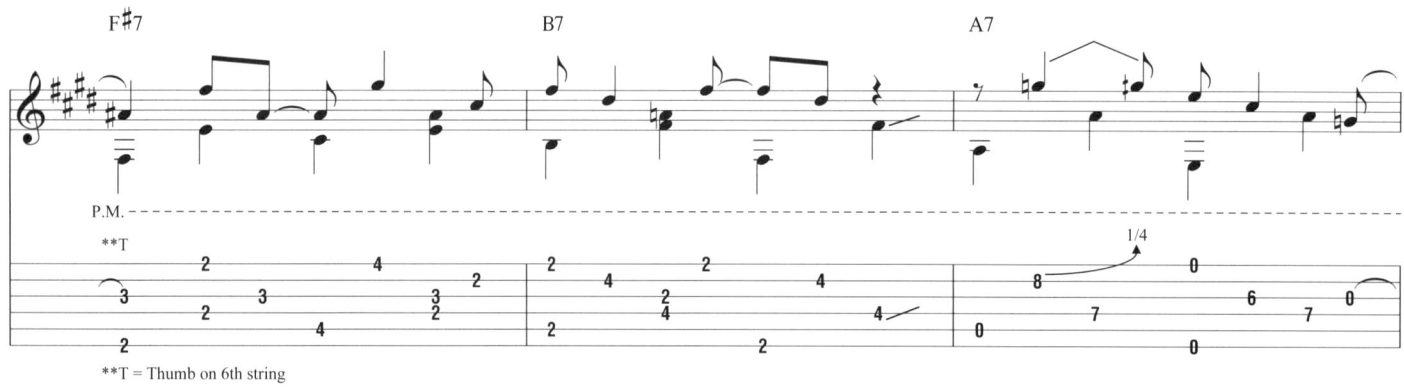

**T = Thumb on 6th string

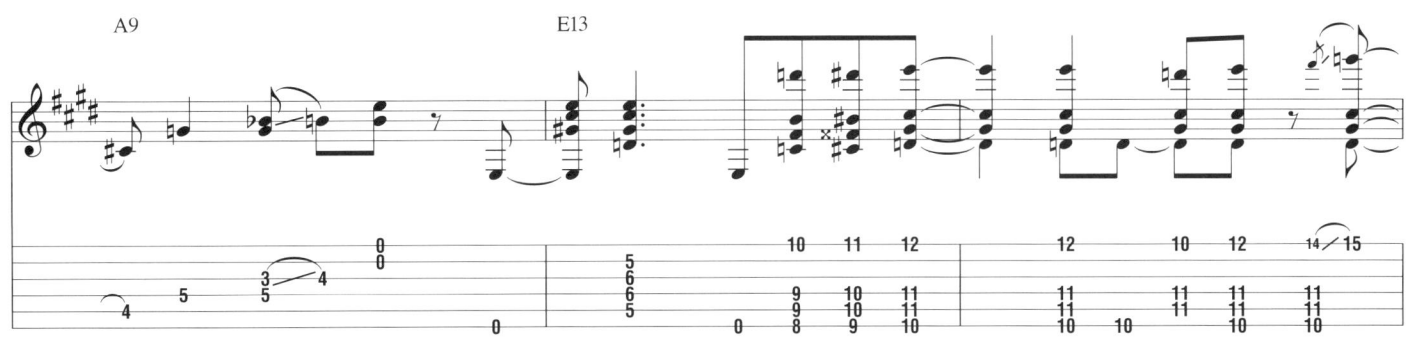
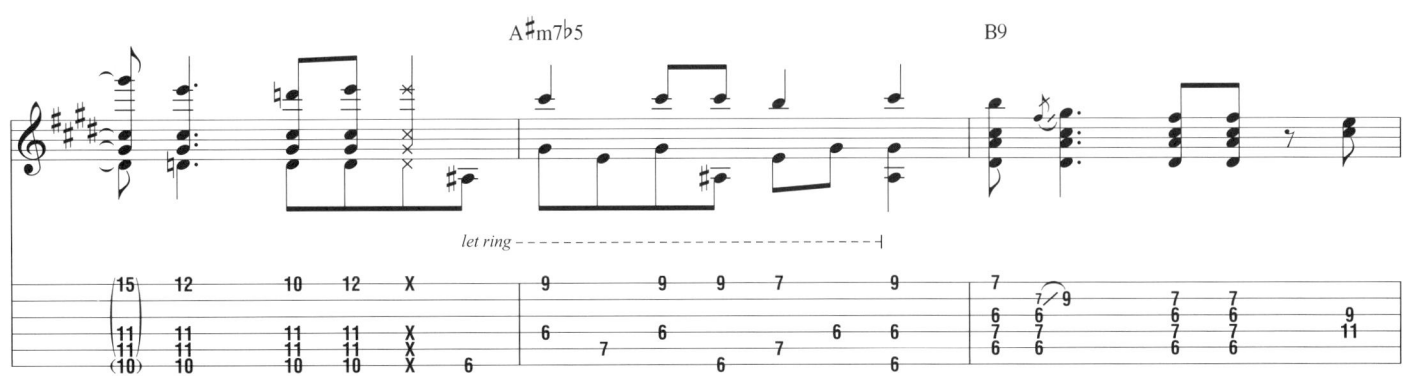

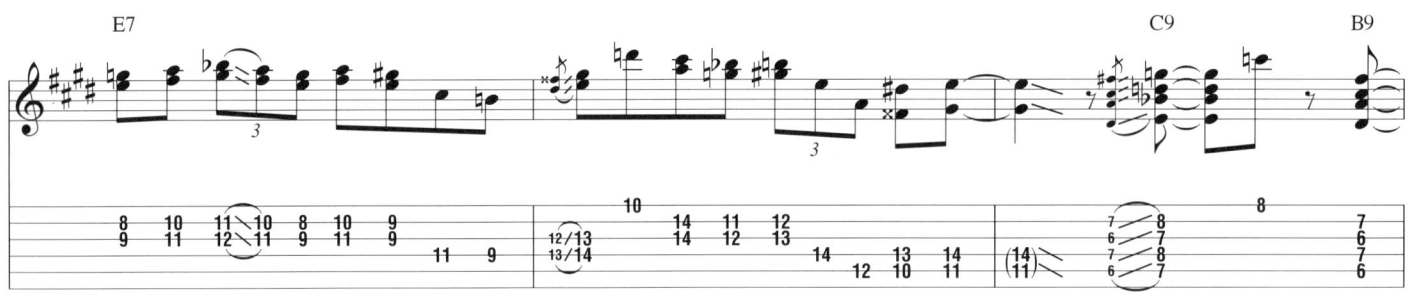

*As before

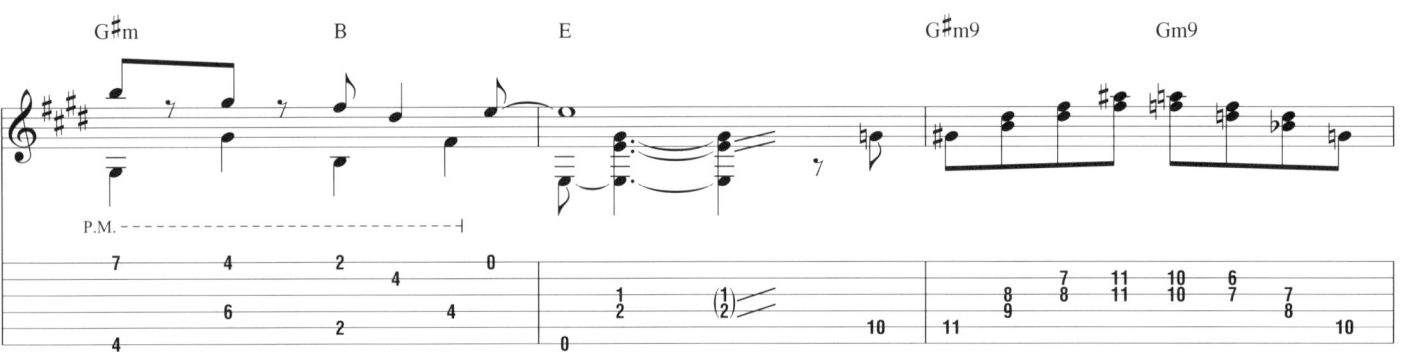

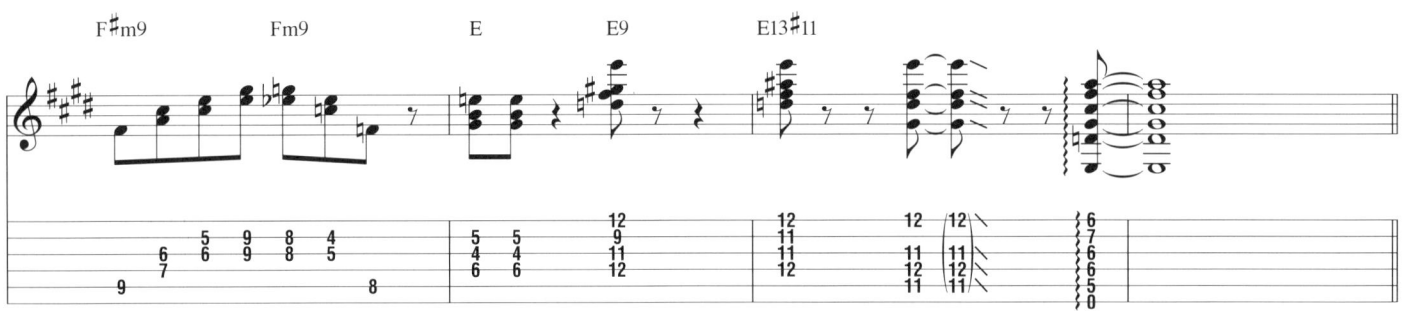

Example 41
(1:09)

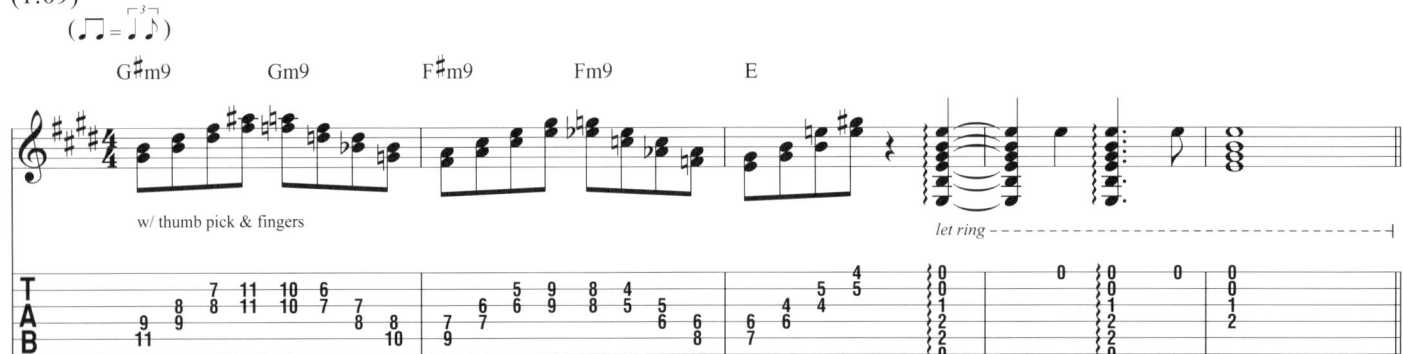

Example 42
(2:32)

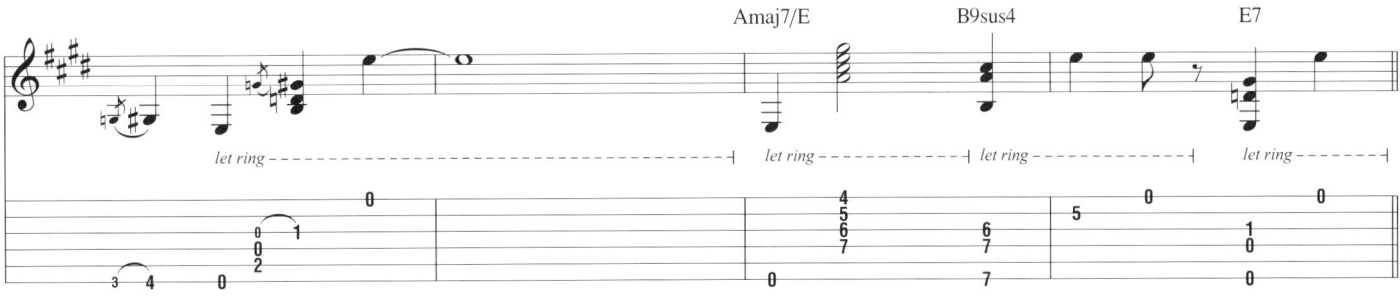

Example 43
(3:15)

Chapter 8: Scales, Licks, Runs and Rhythms

Example 44
(:14)

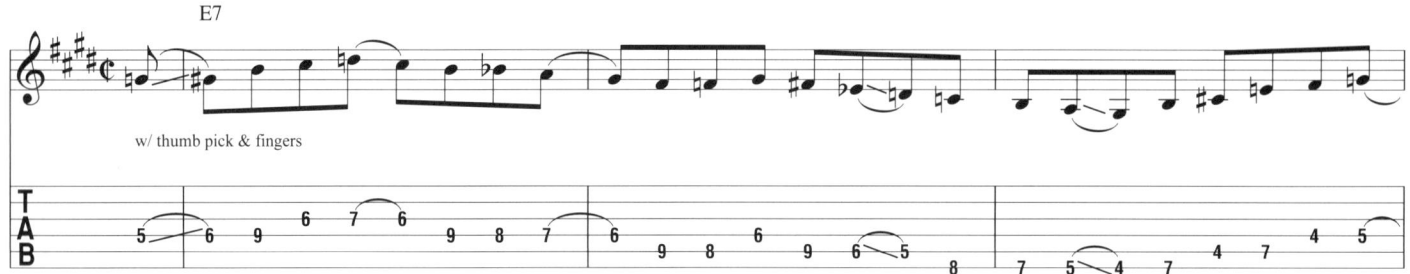

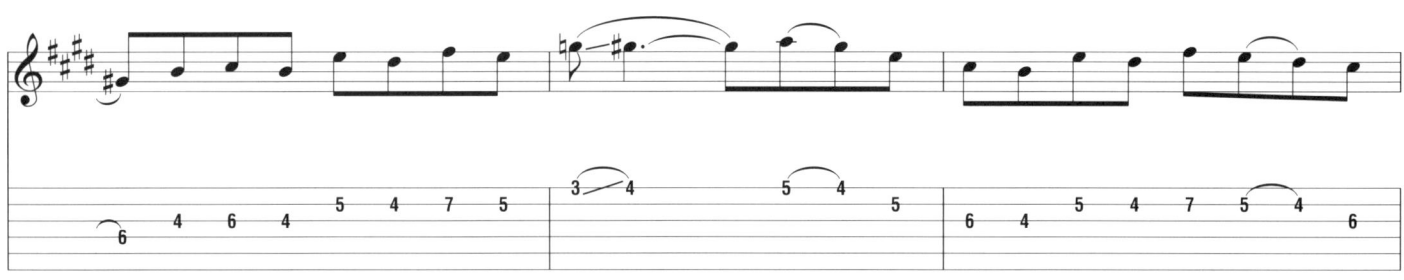

Example 45
(:21)

Example 46
(:44)

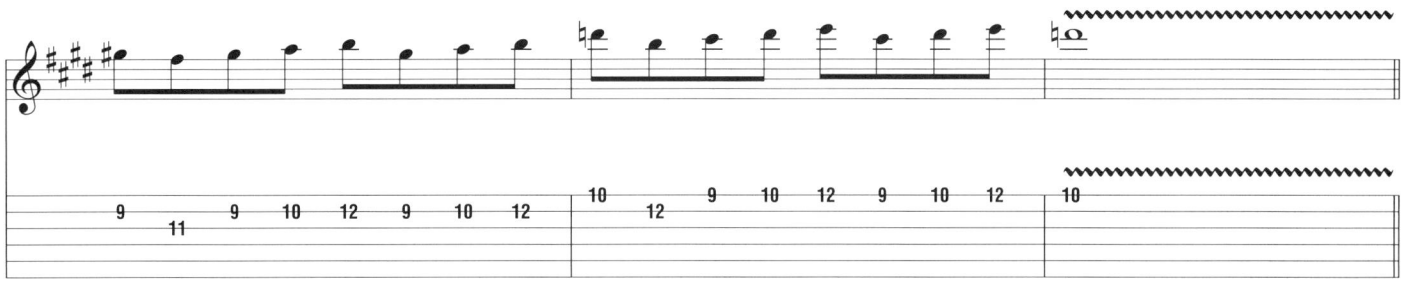

Example 47
(1:05)

Example 48
(1:25)

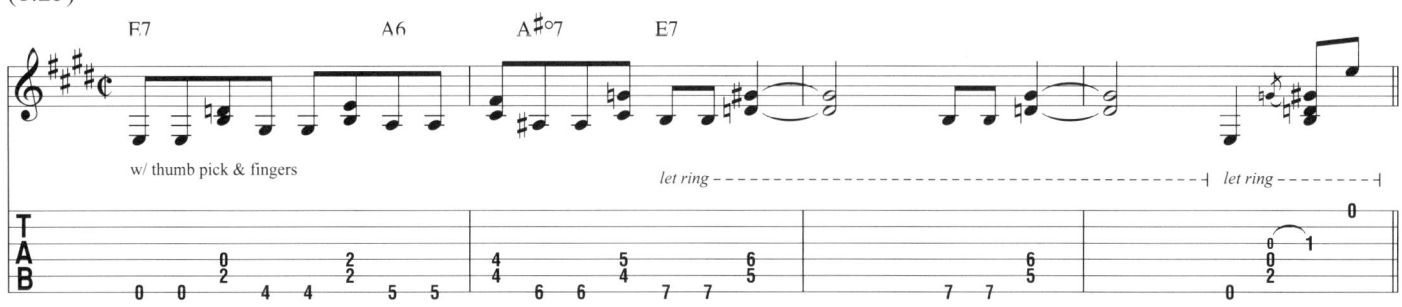

Example 49
(1:44)

Example 50
(2:14)

Example 51
(2:36)

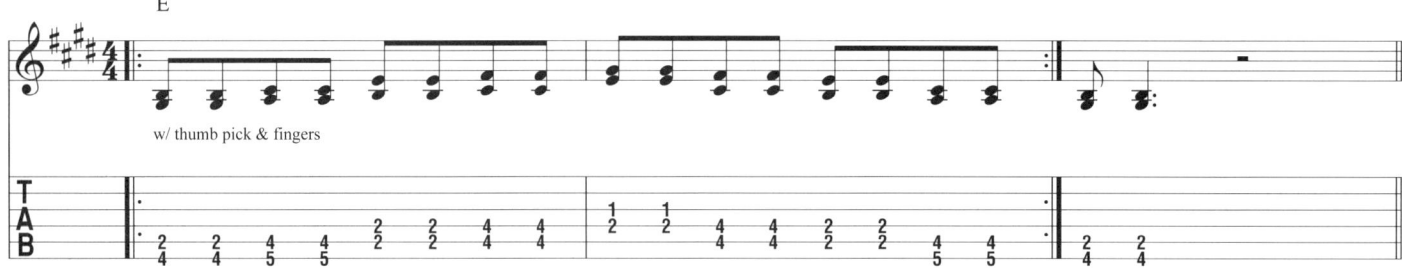

Example 52
(2:52)

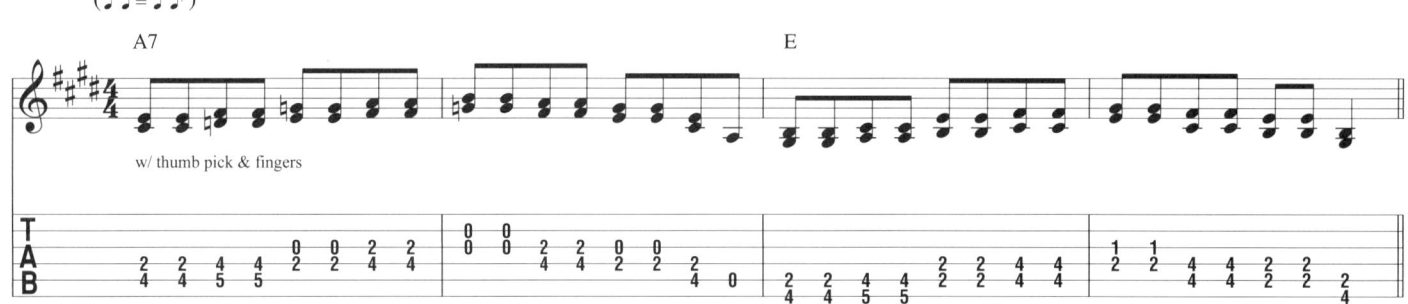

Example 53
(3:14)

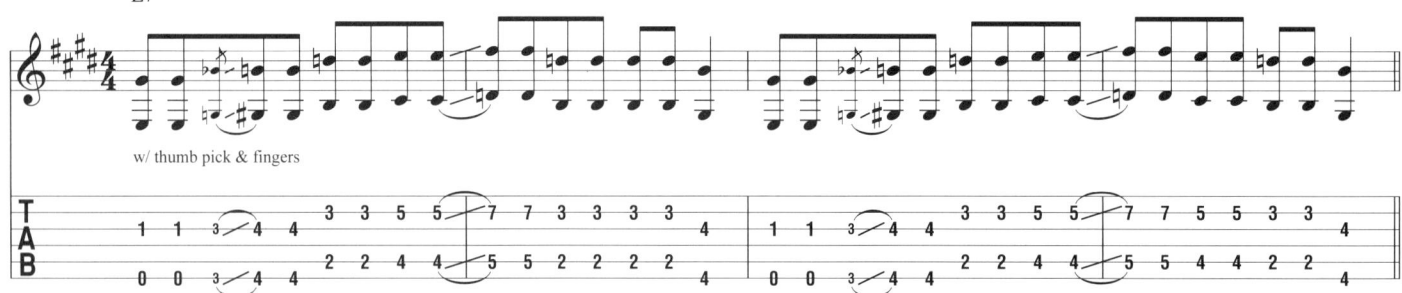

Chapter 9: Chord-Based Double Stops and Riffs

Example 54
(:14)

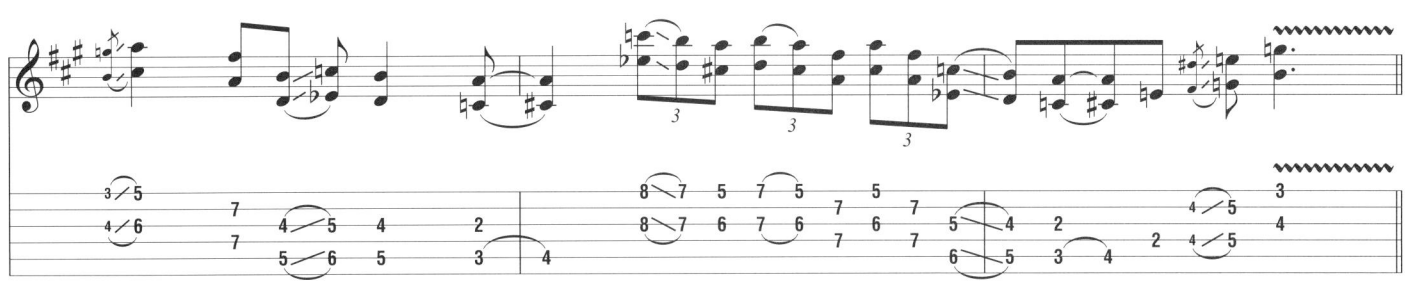

Example 55

Example 56

(1:03)

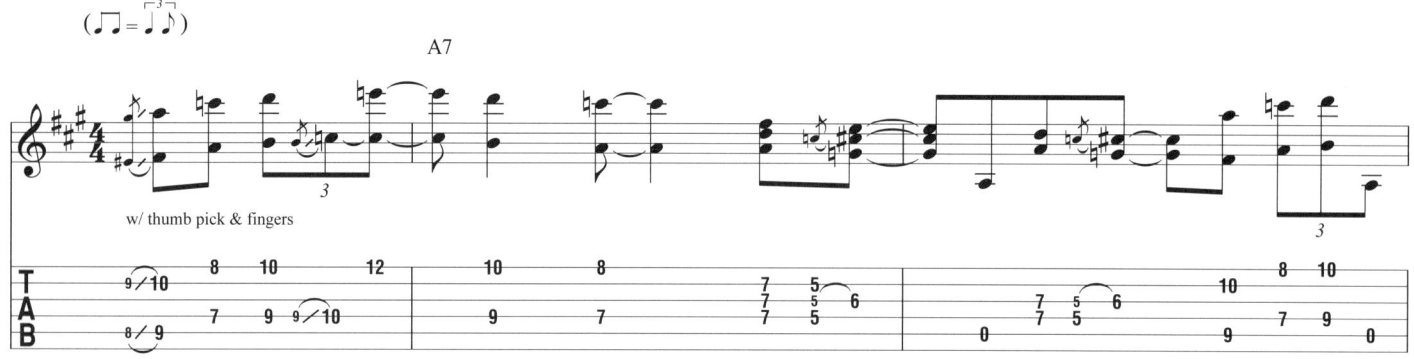

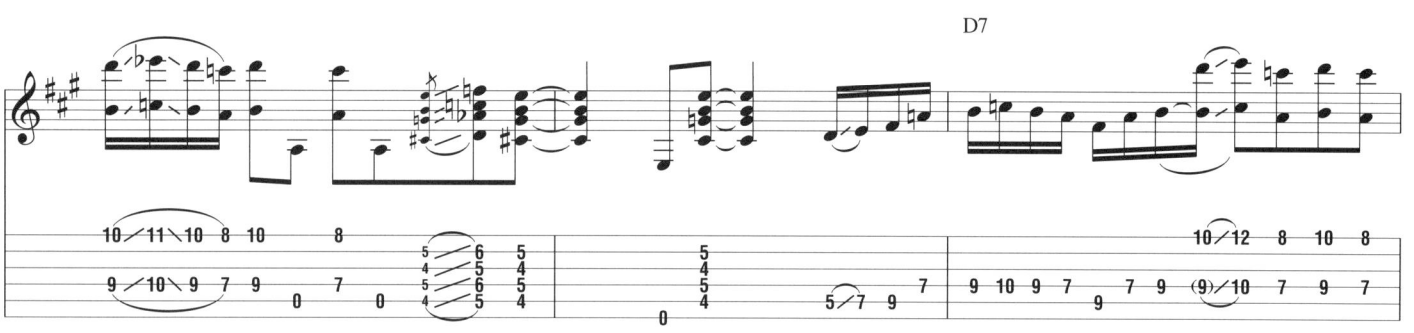

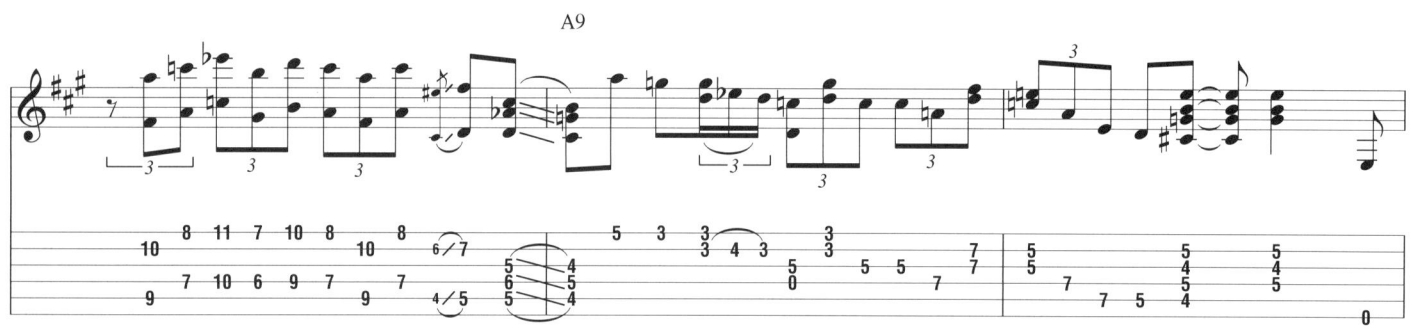

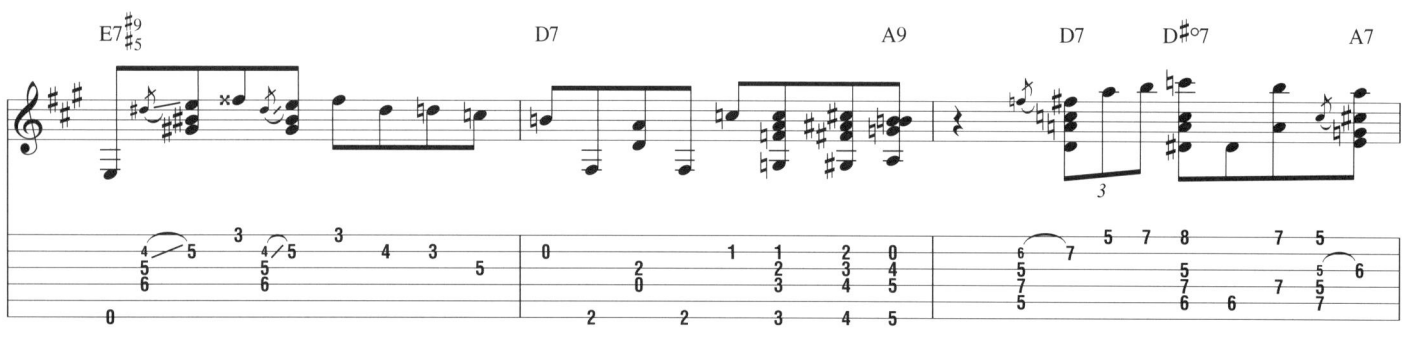

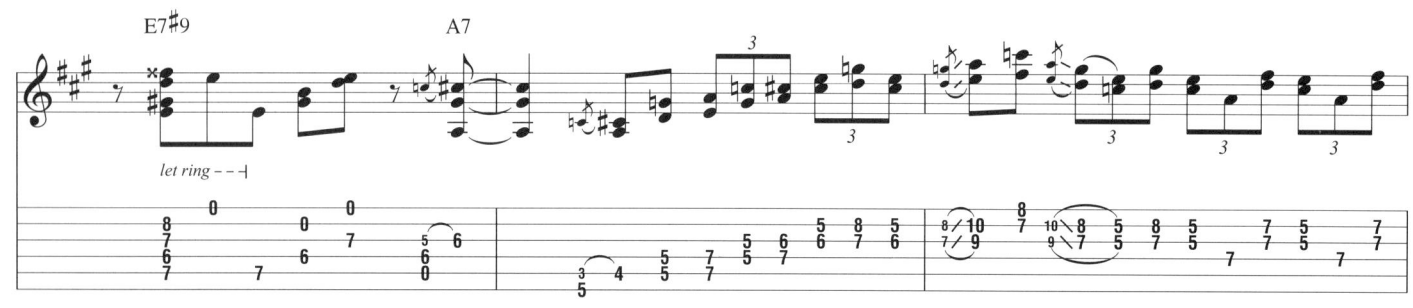

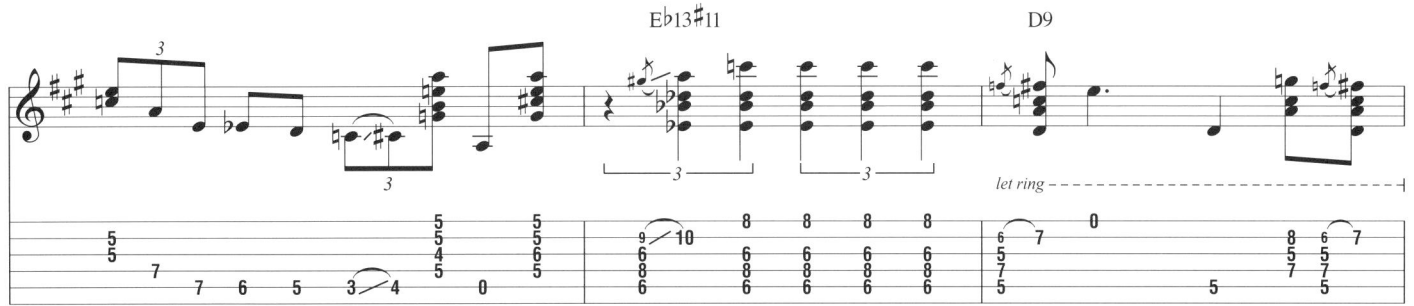
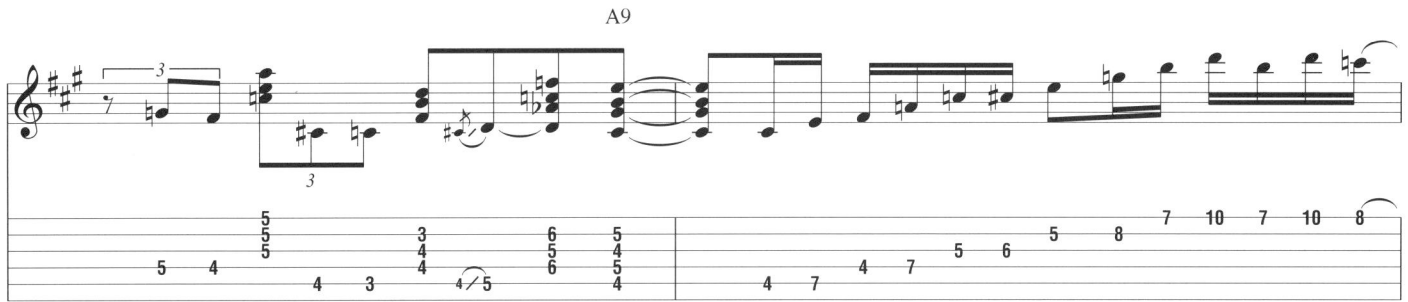
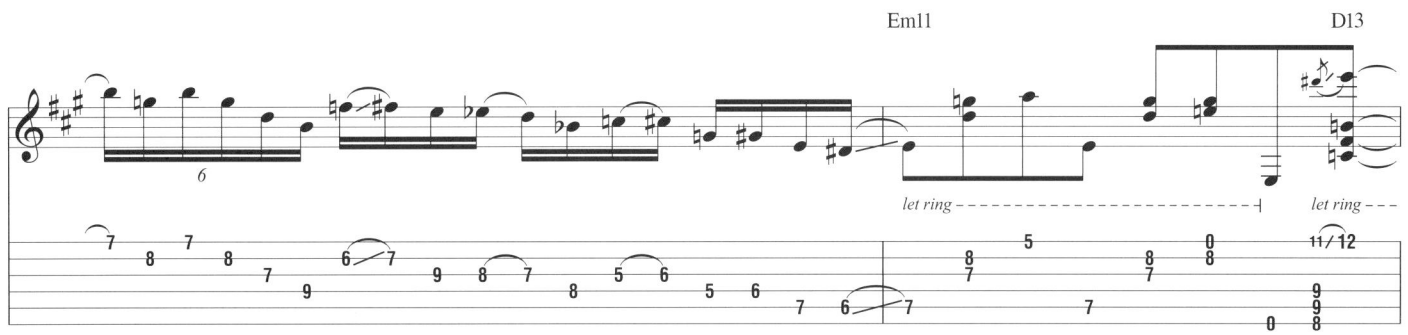
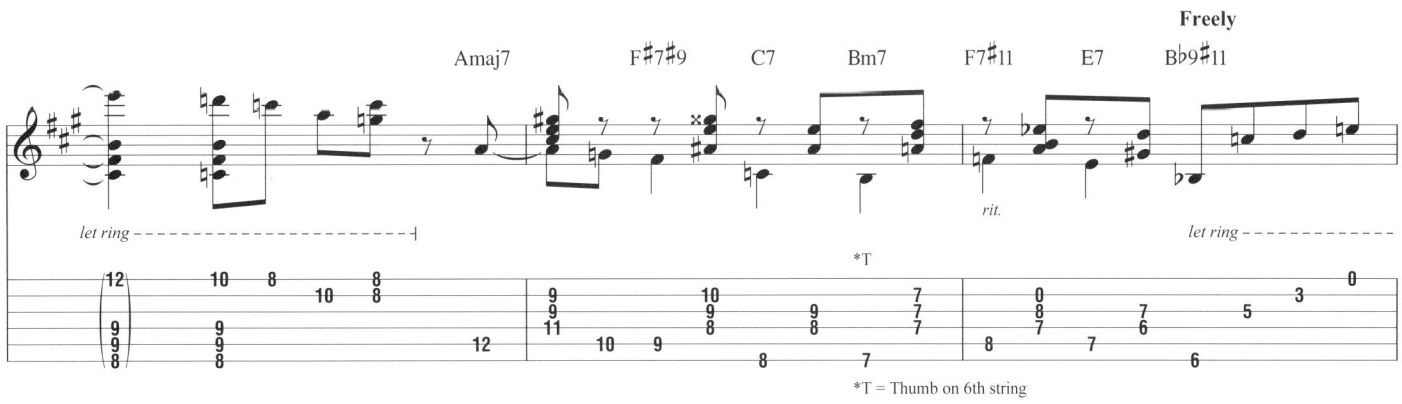

*T = Thumb on 6th string

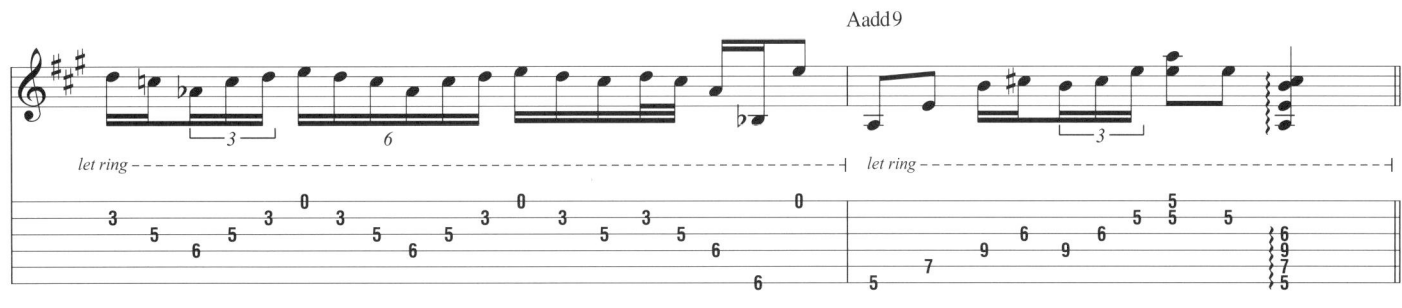

35

Example 57
(2:16)

Example 58
(2:44)

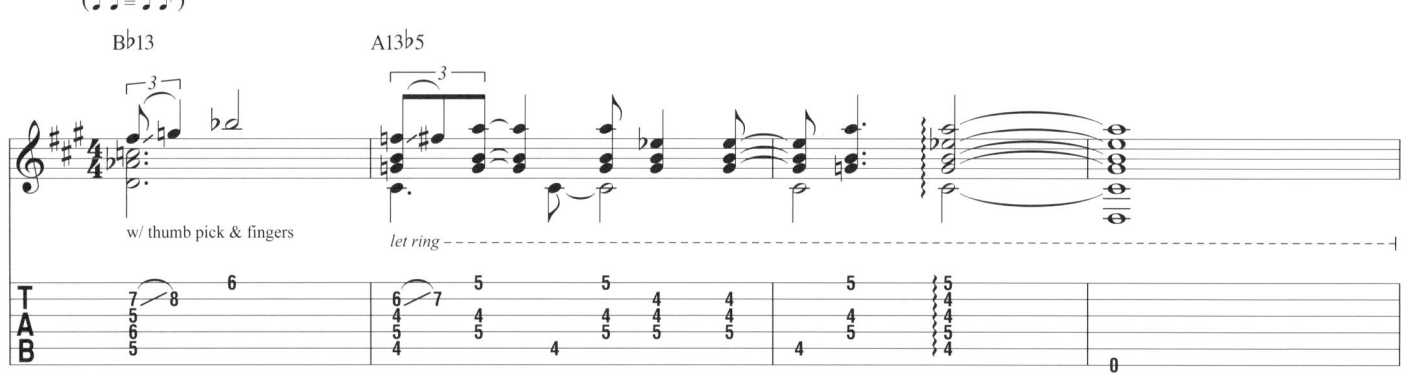

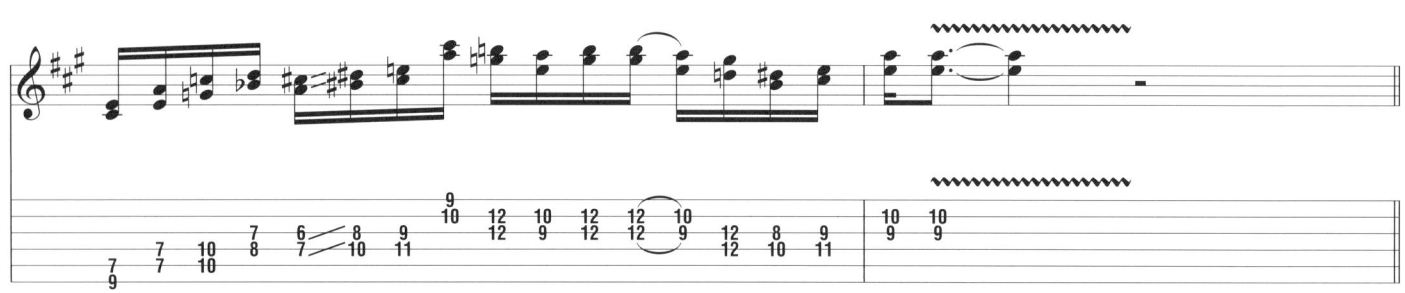

Example 59
(3:21)

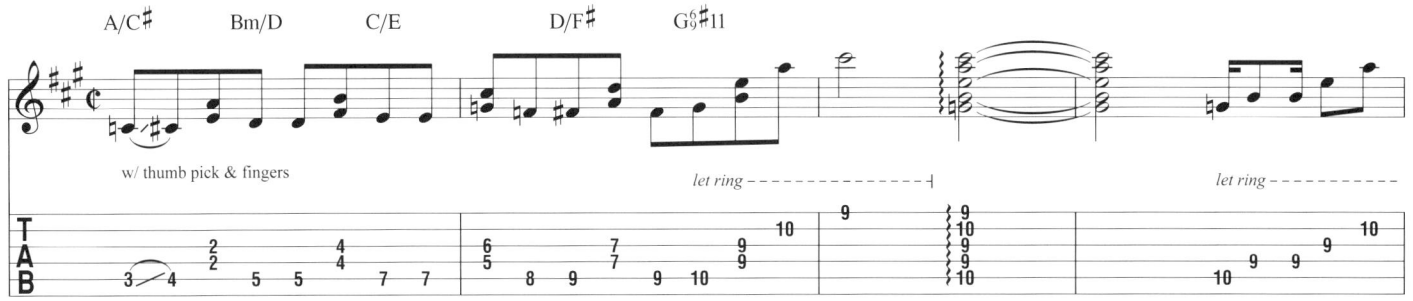

Example 60
(3:43)

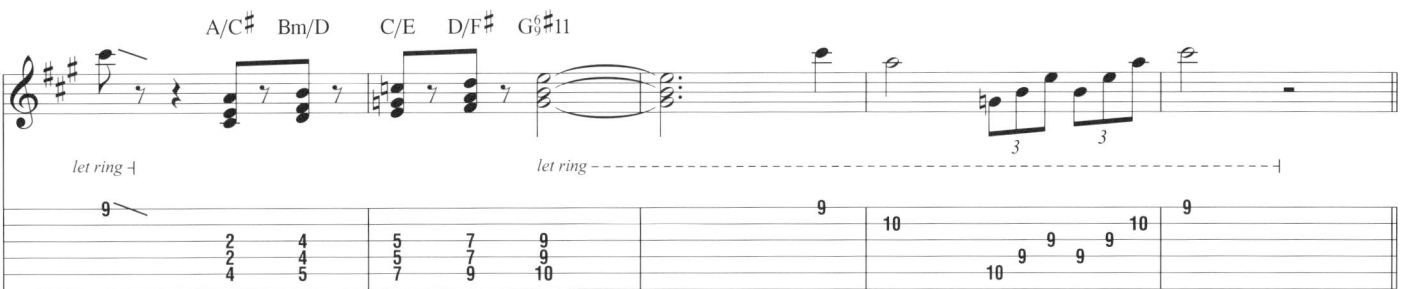

Example 61
(3:56)

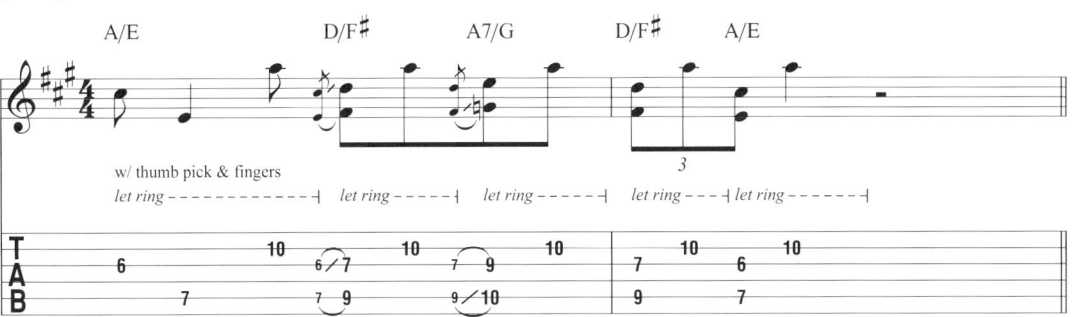

Example 62
(4:14)

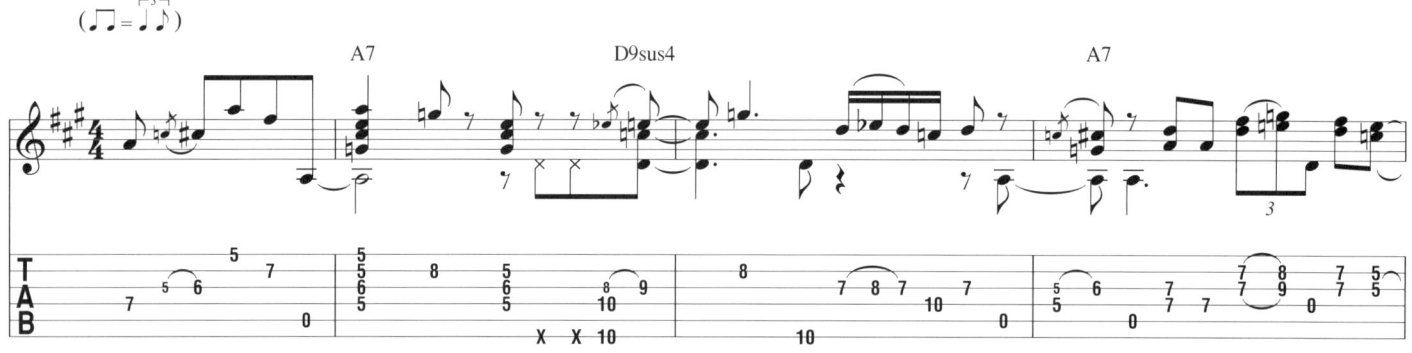

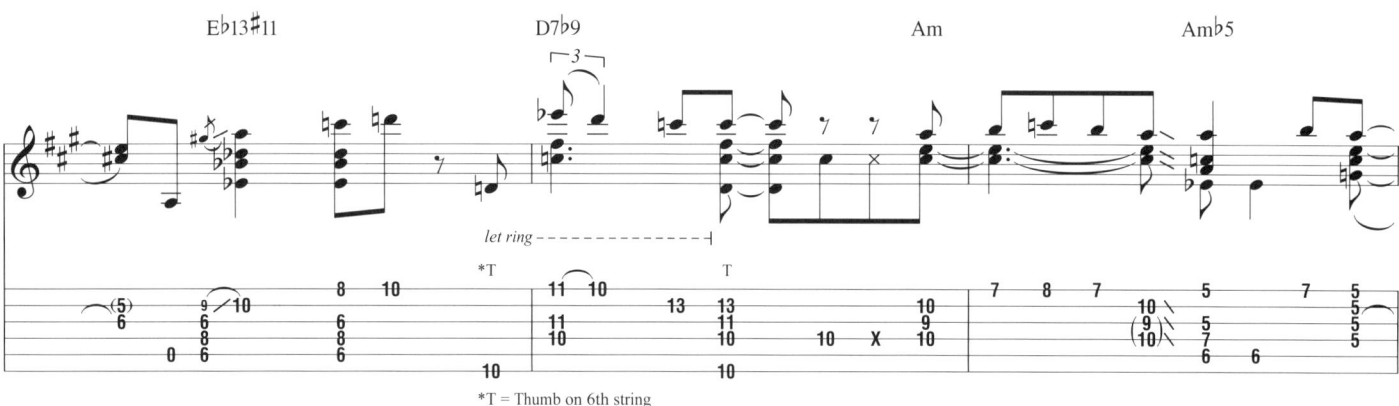

*T = Thumb on 6th string

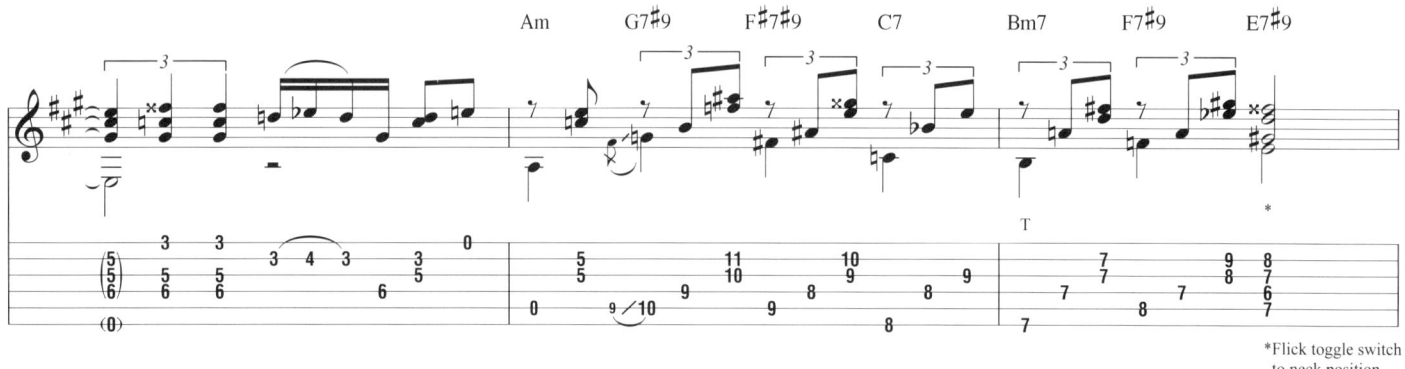

*Flick toggle switch to neck position.

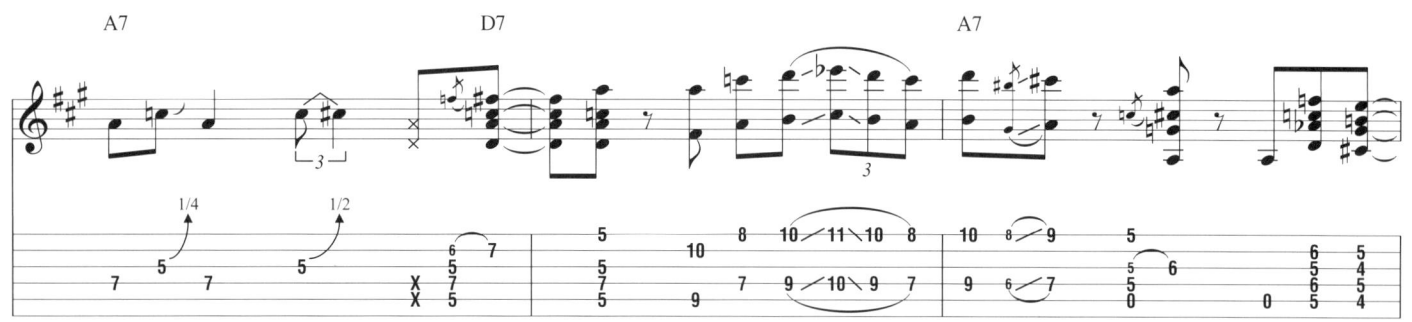

*Flick toggle switch.

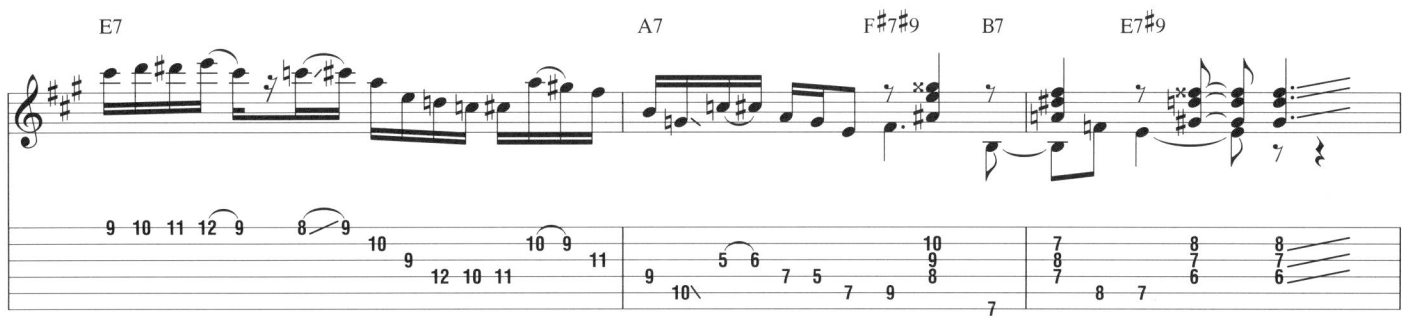

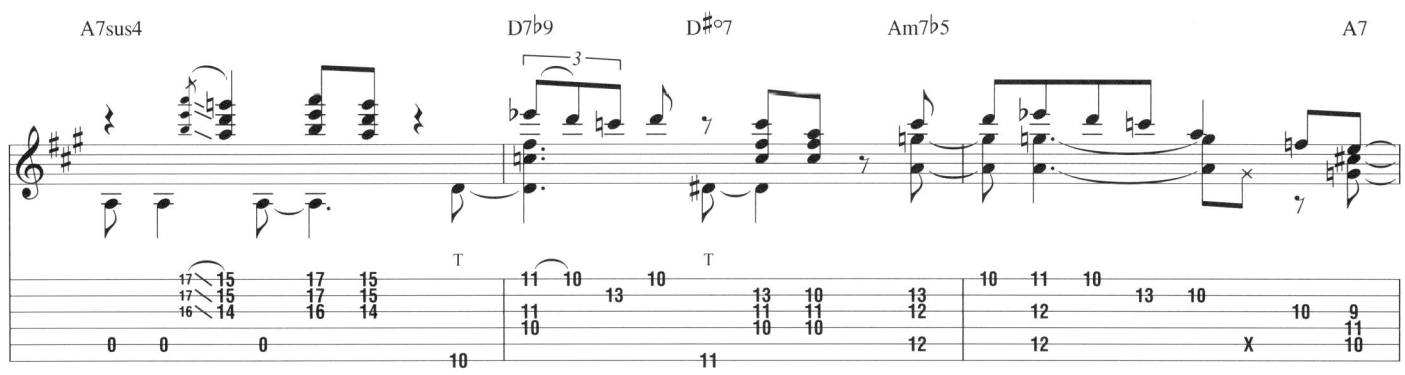

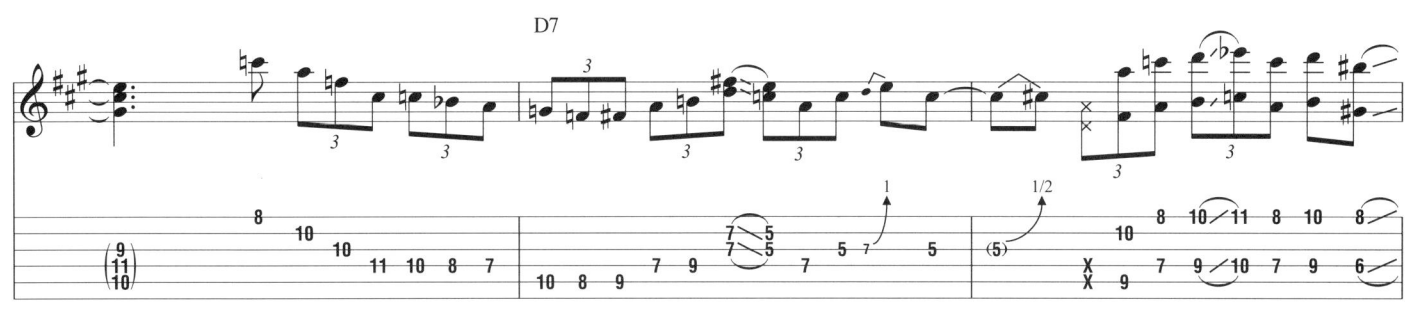

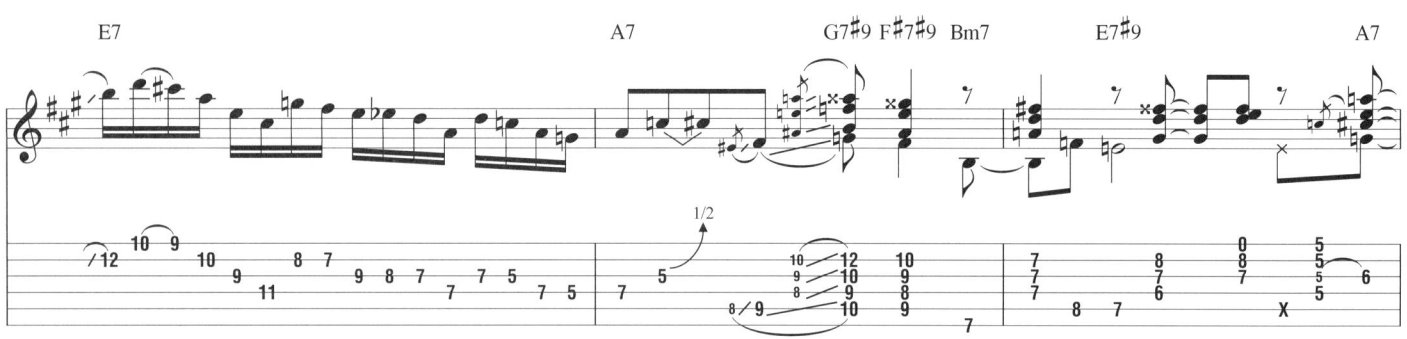
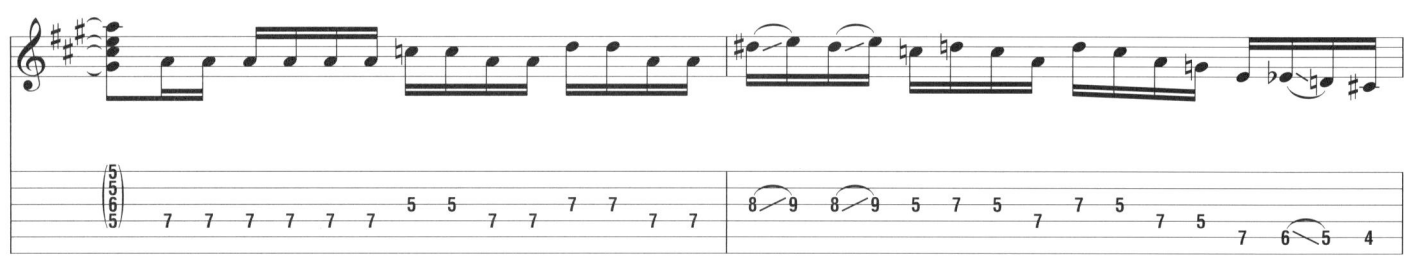

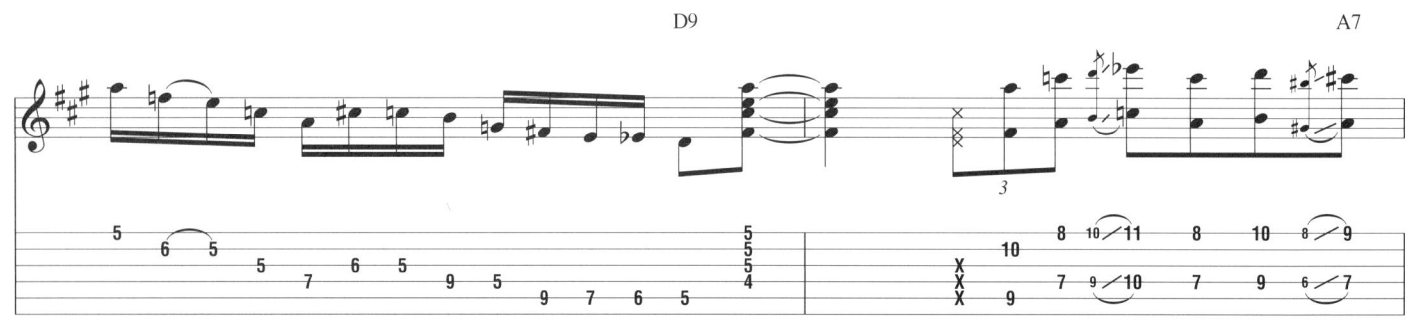

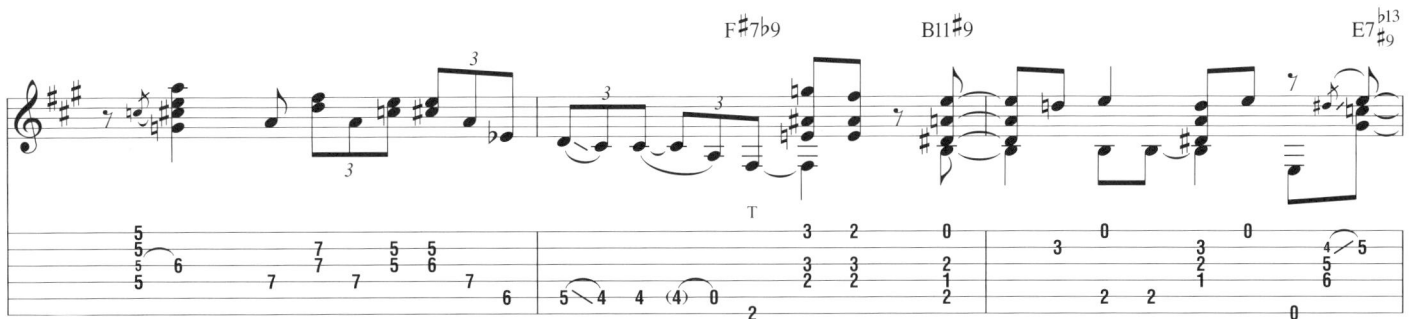

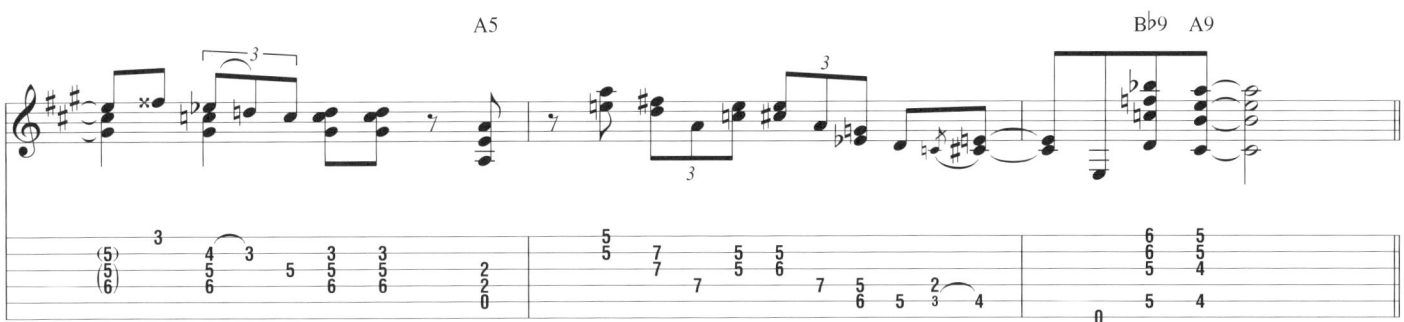

Example 63
(5:30)

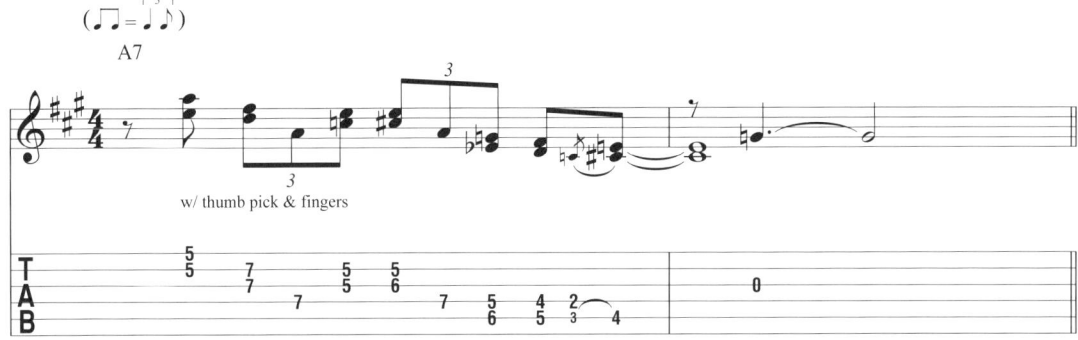

Example 64
(5:43)

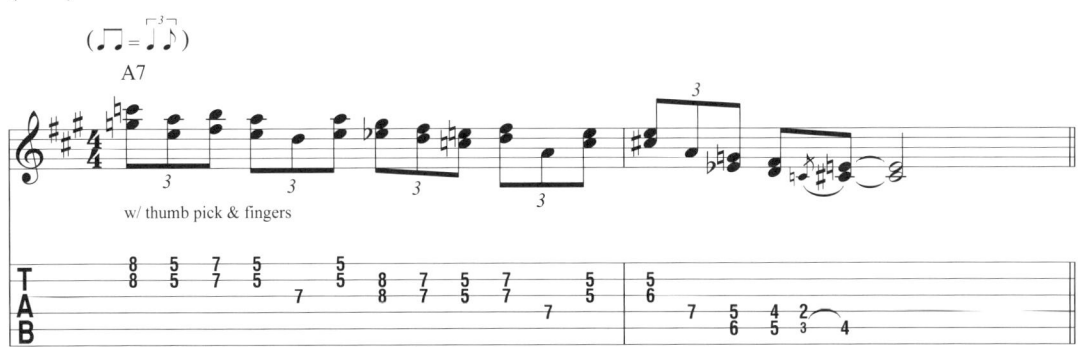

Chapter 10: Chet Atkins-Style Performance

Example 65
(:05)

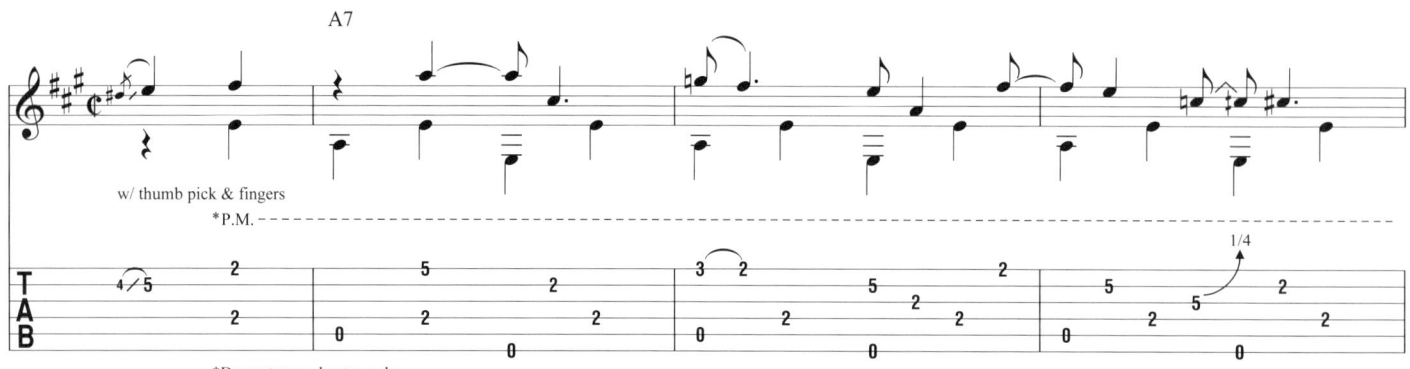

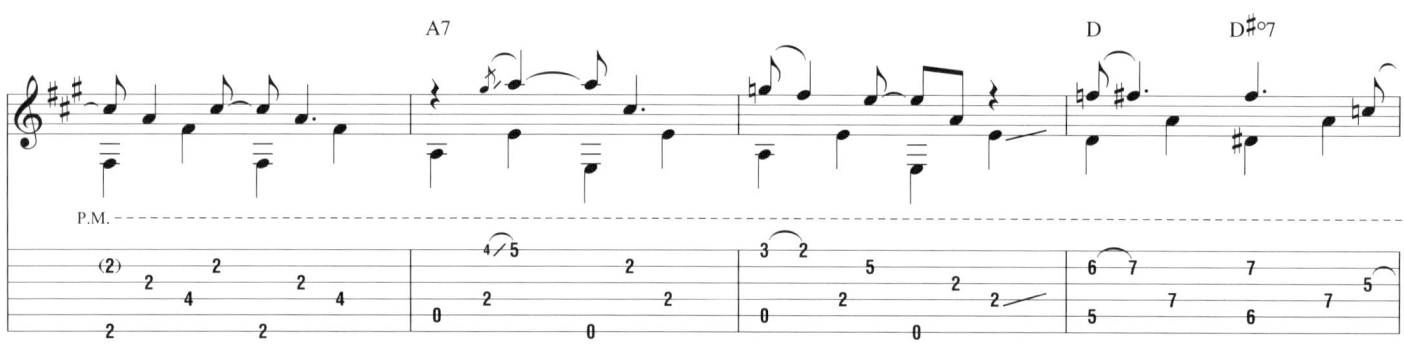

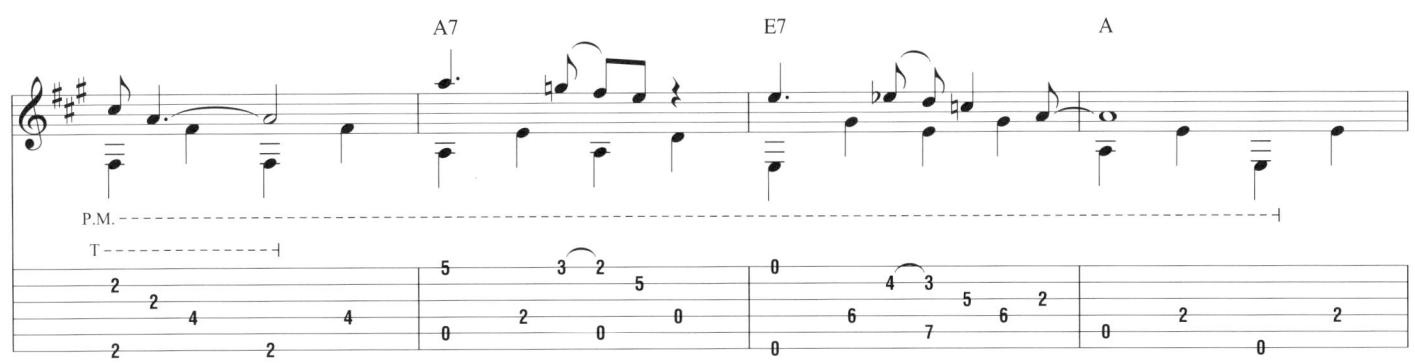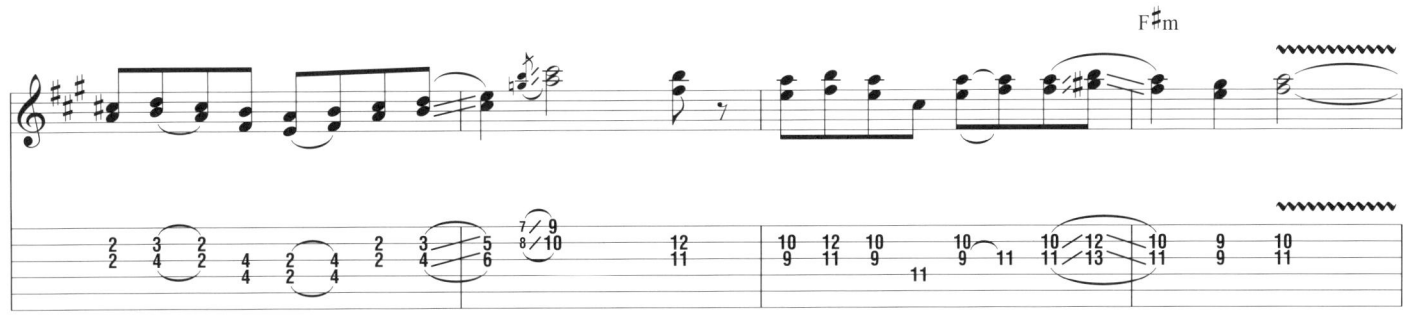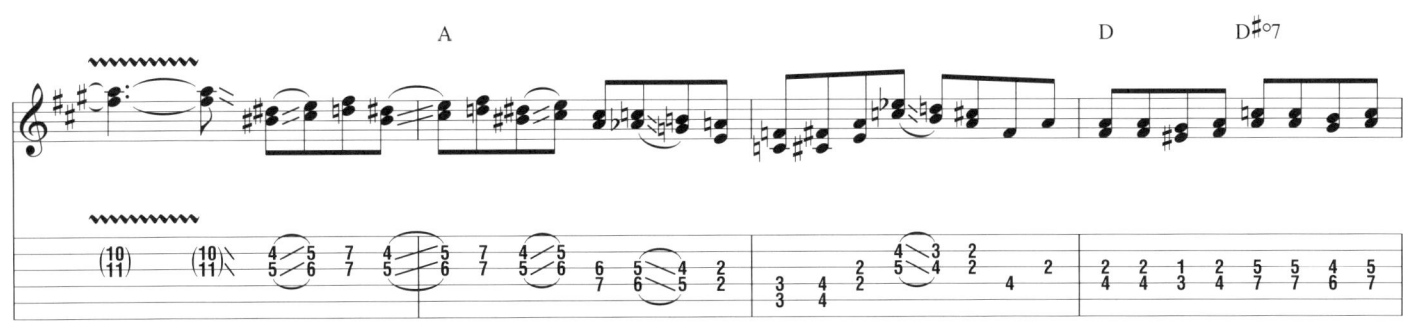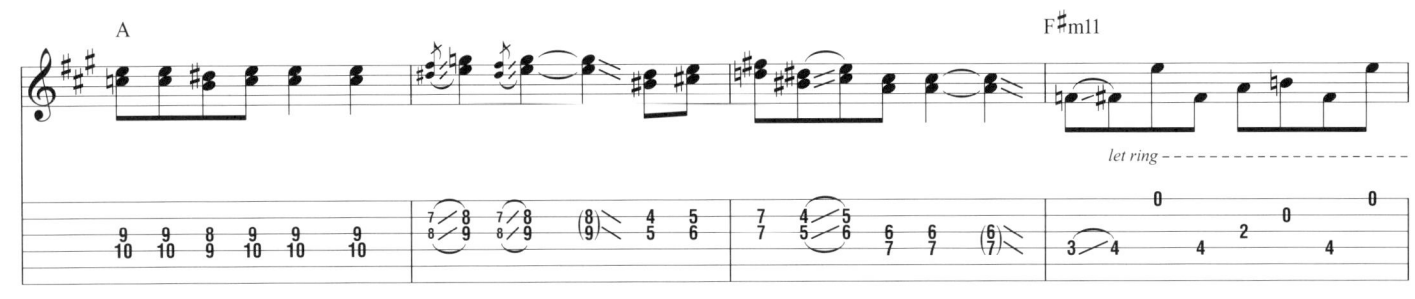

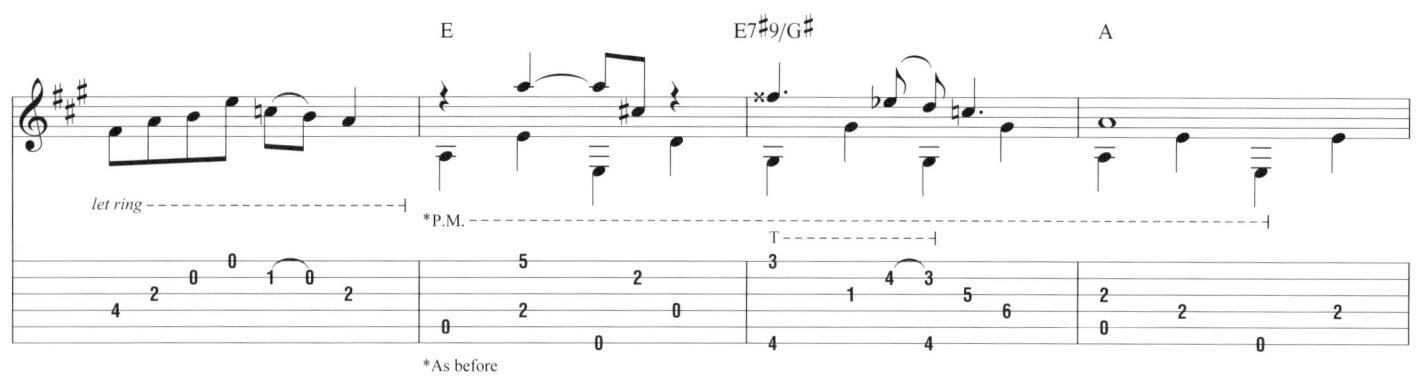
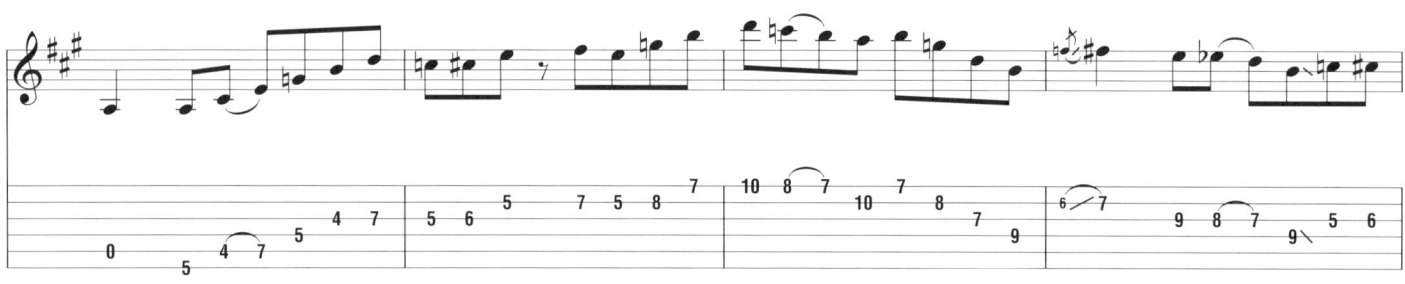
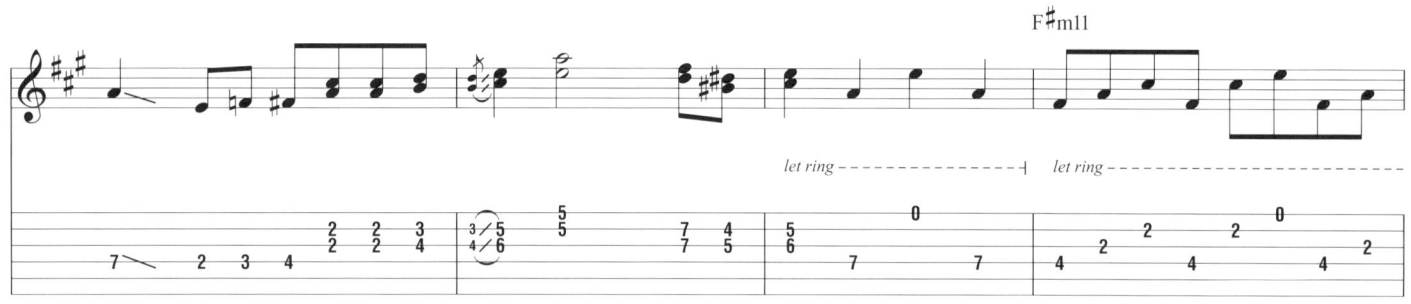
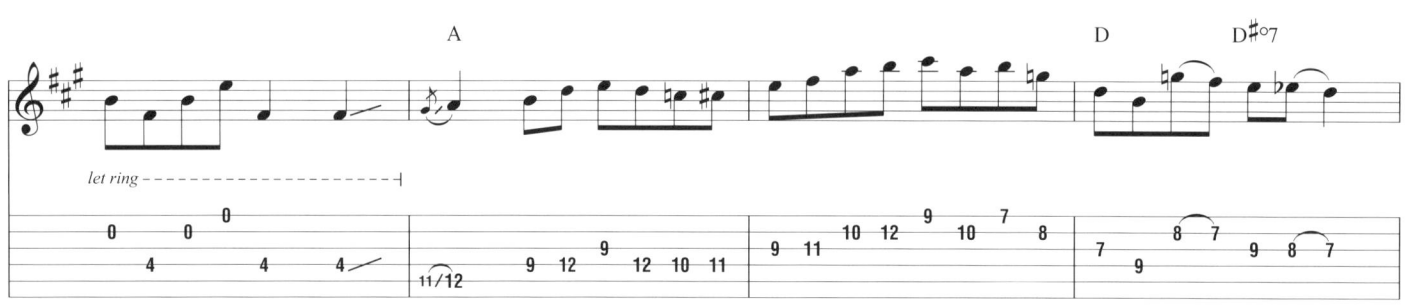
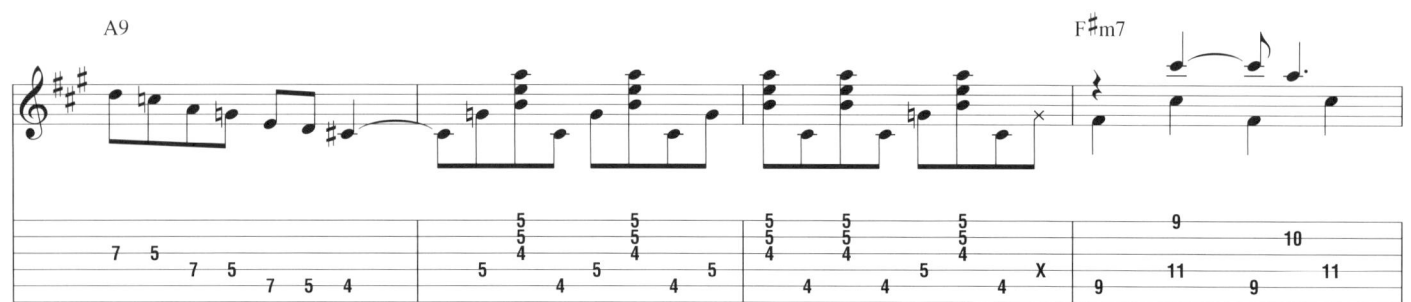

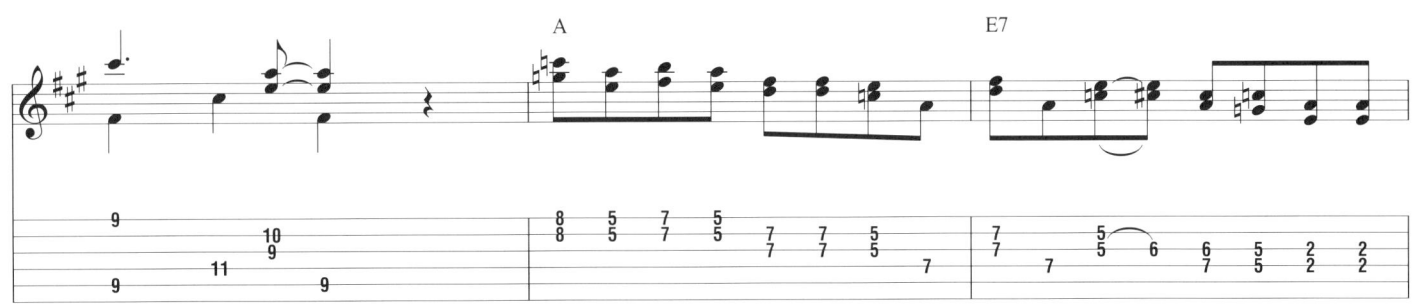

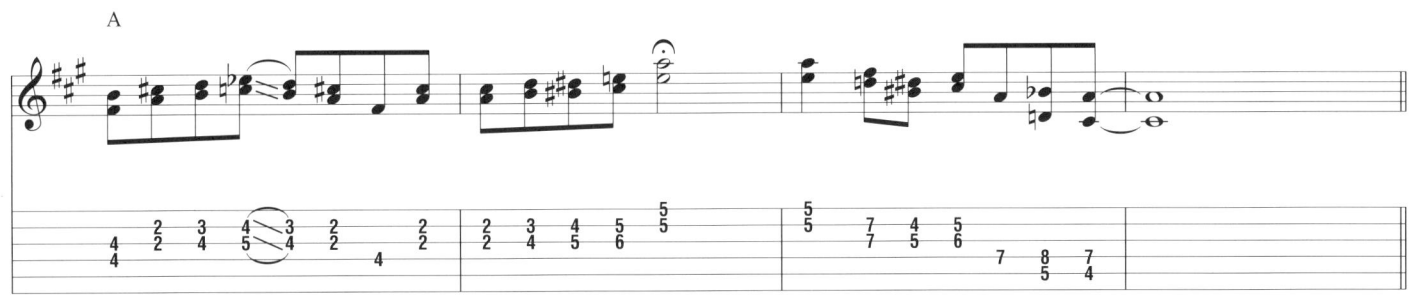

Example 66
(1:27)

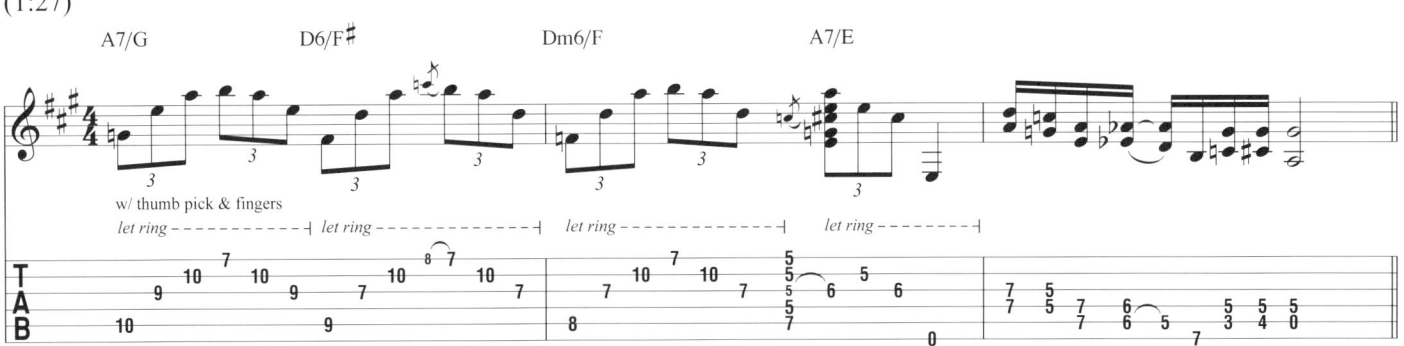

Example 67
(1:44)

45

Example 68
(1:56)

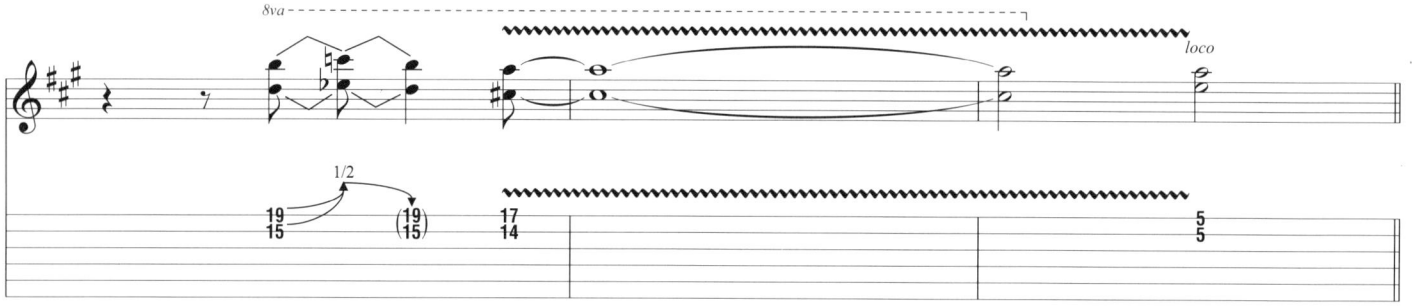

Example 69
(2:12)

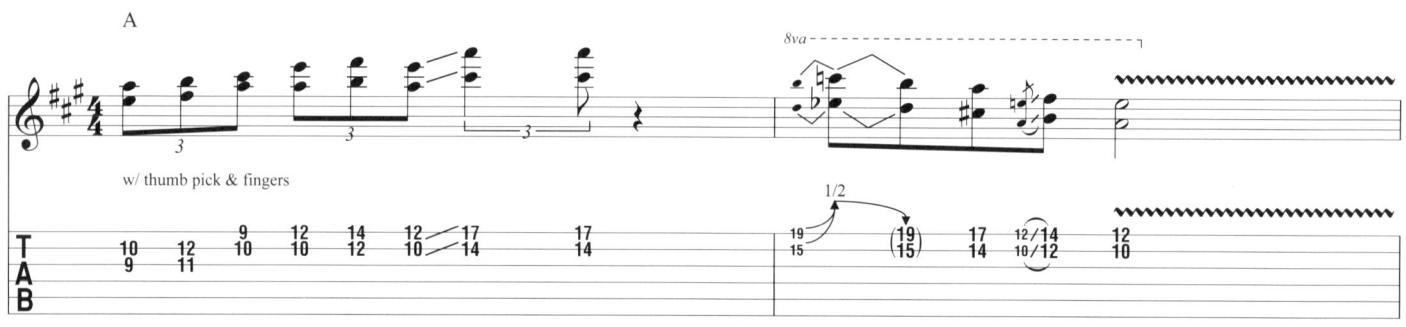

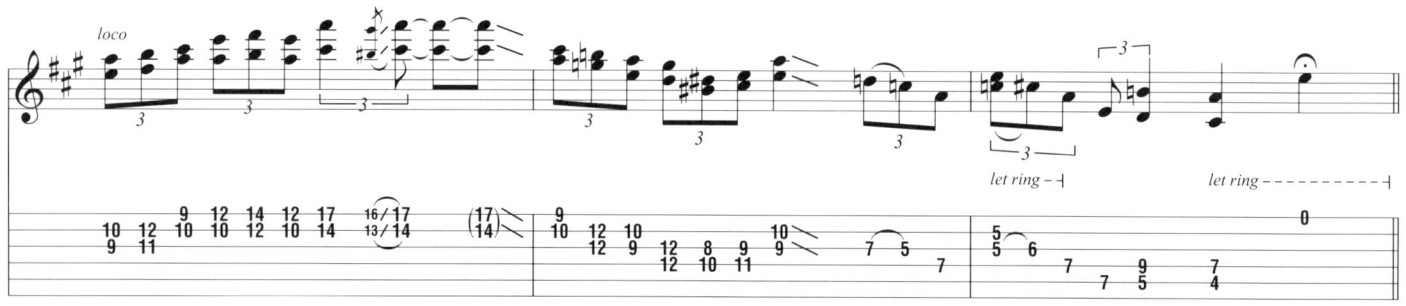

Example 70
(2:50)

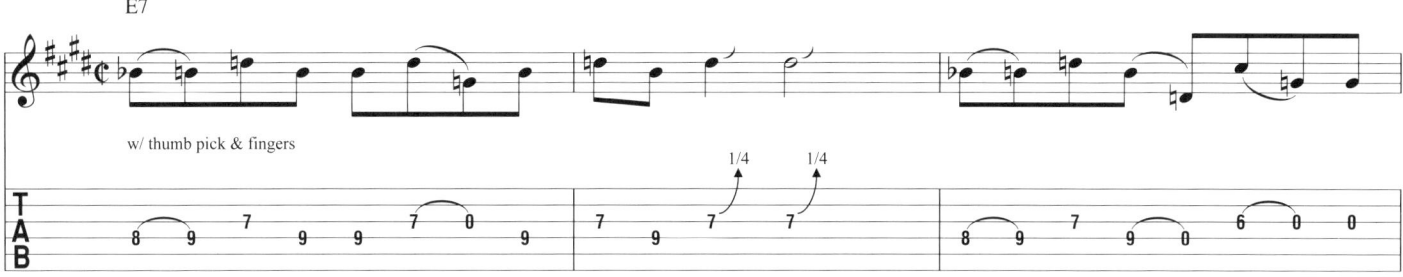

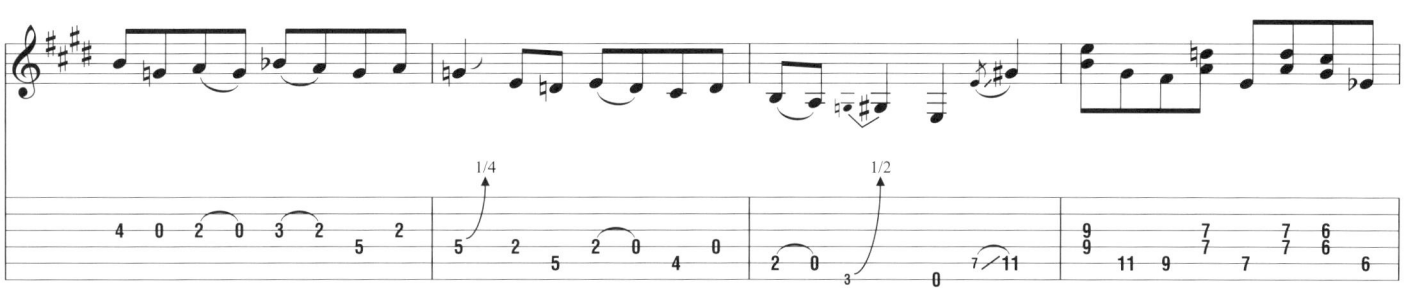

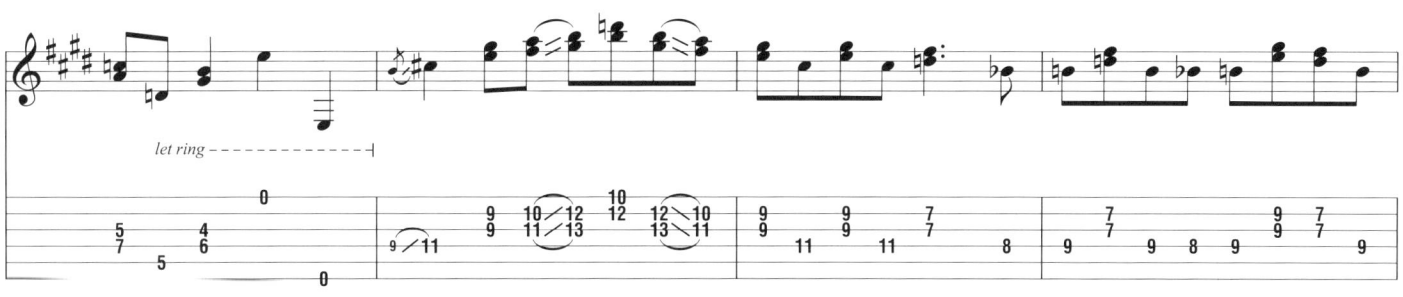

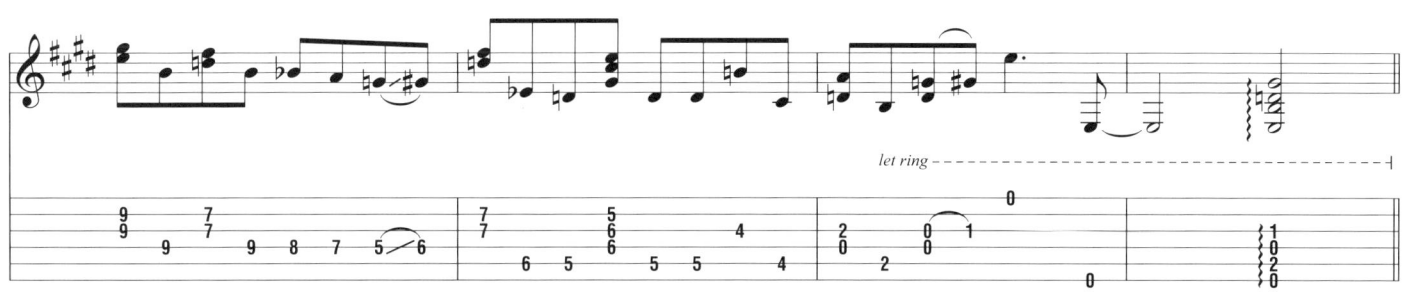

Example 71
(3:11)

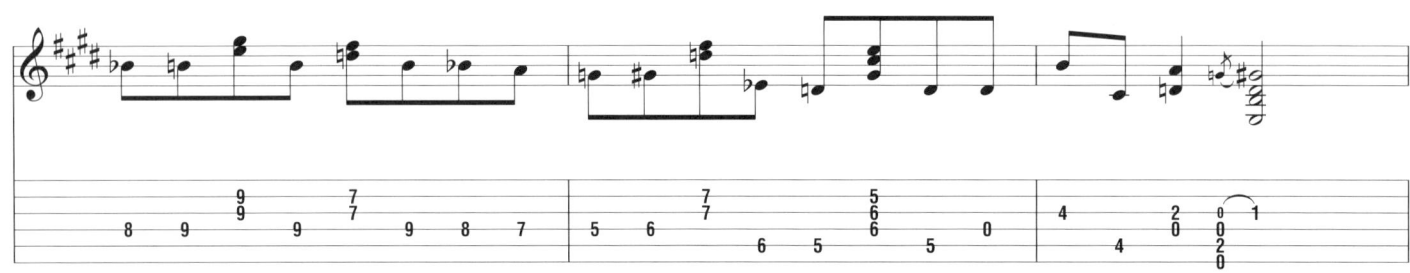
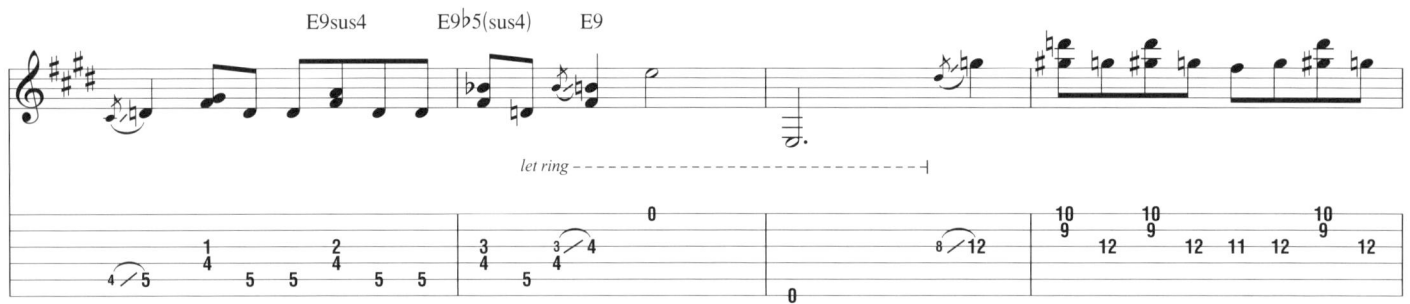

Example 72
(3:37)

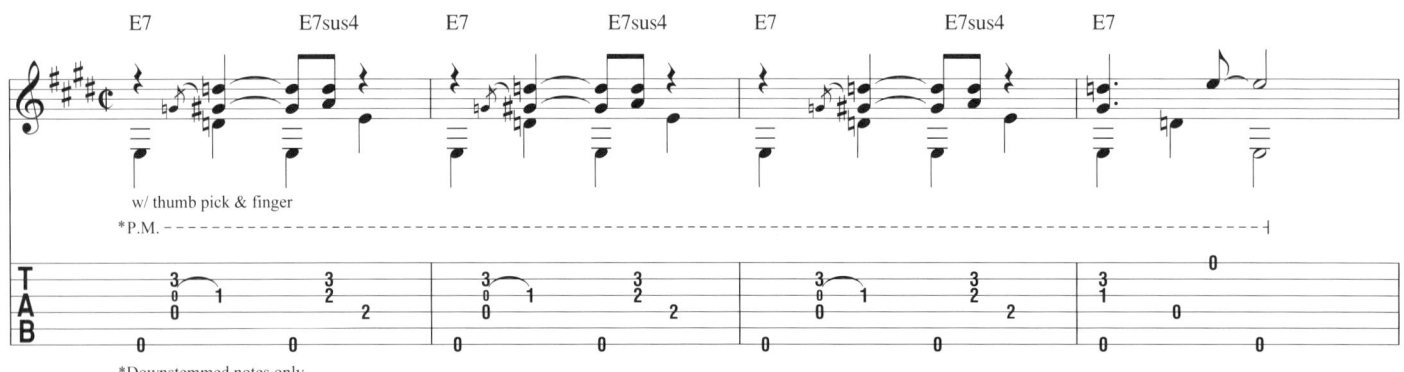

*Downstemmed notes only.

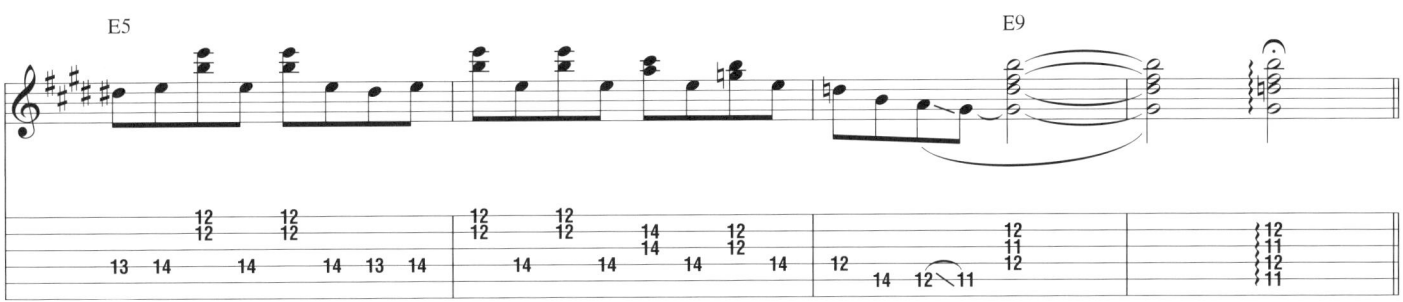

Example 73
(4:25)

w/ thumb pick & fingers

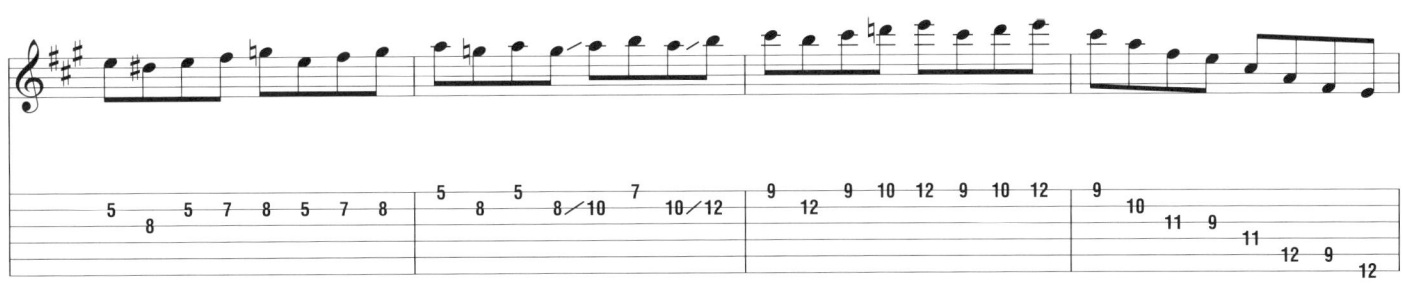

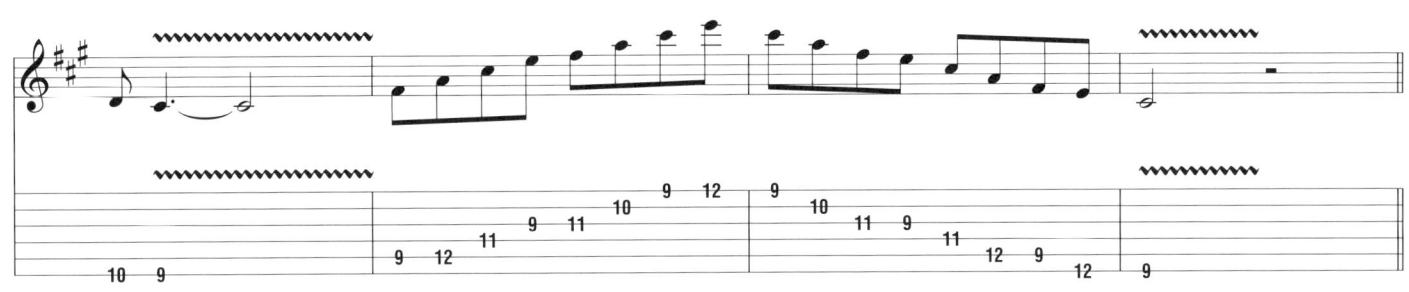

Example 74
(4:43)

Chapter 11: Chord Melody

Example 75
(:22)

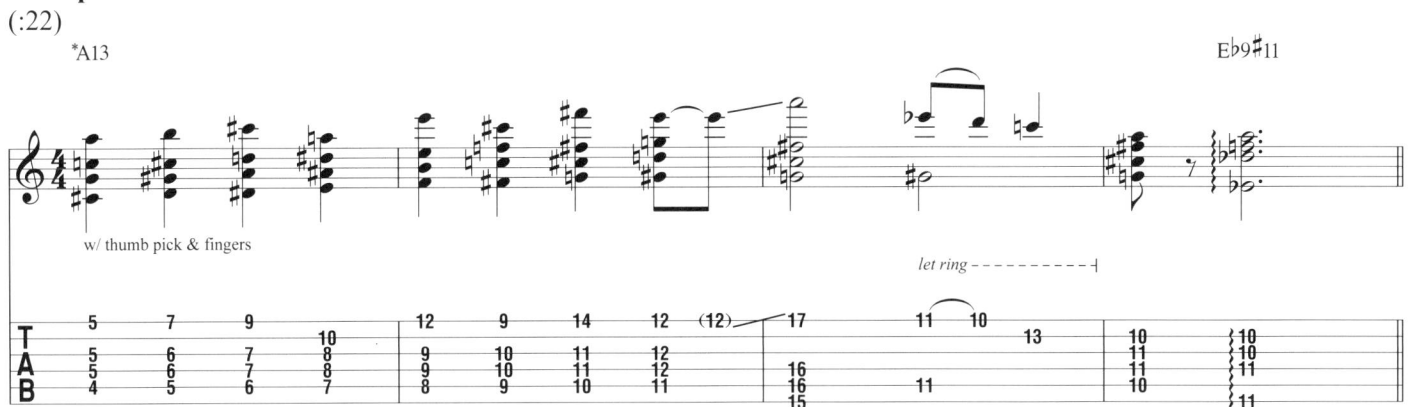

*Chord symbols reflect basic harmony.

Example 76
(:30)

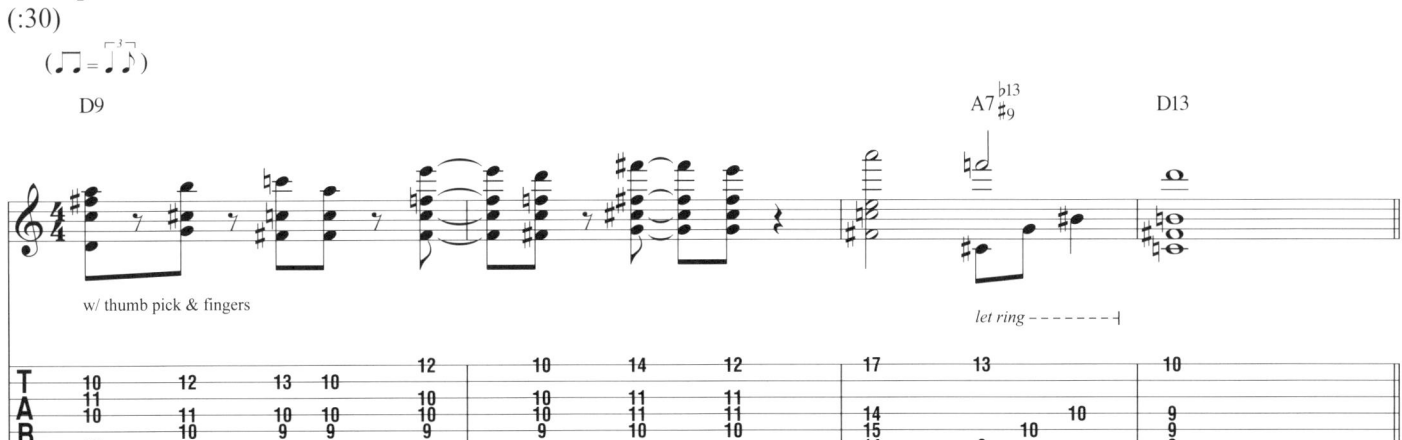

Example 77
(:36)

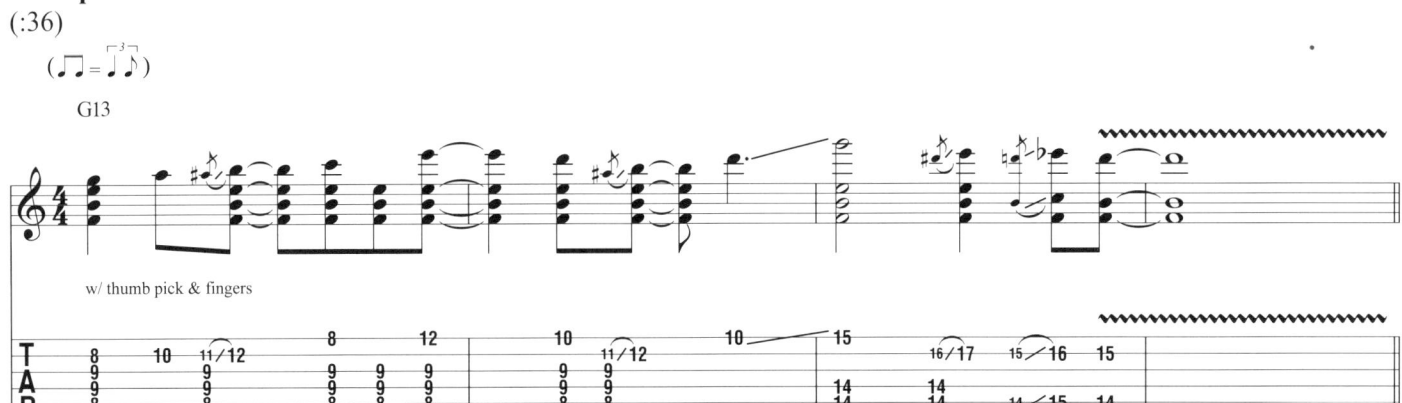

Example 78
(:42)

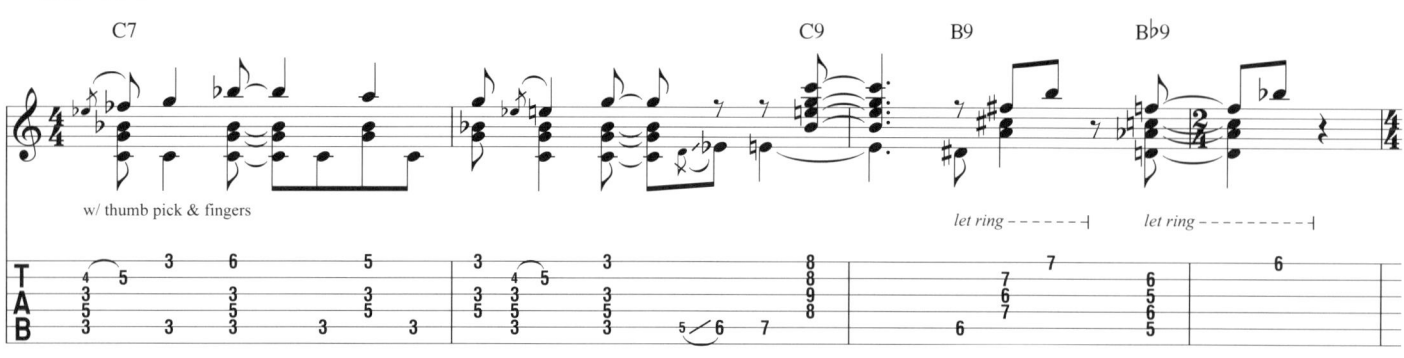

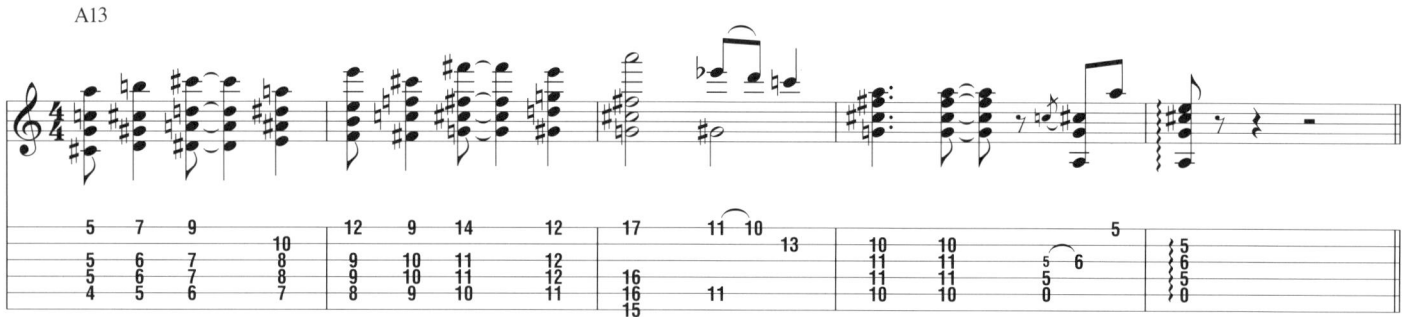

Example 79
(:51)

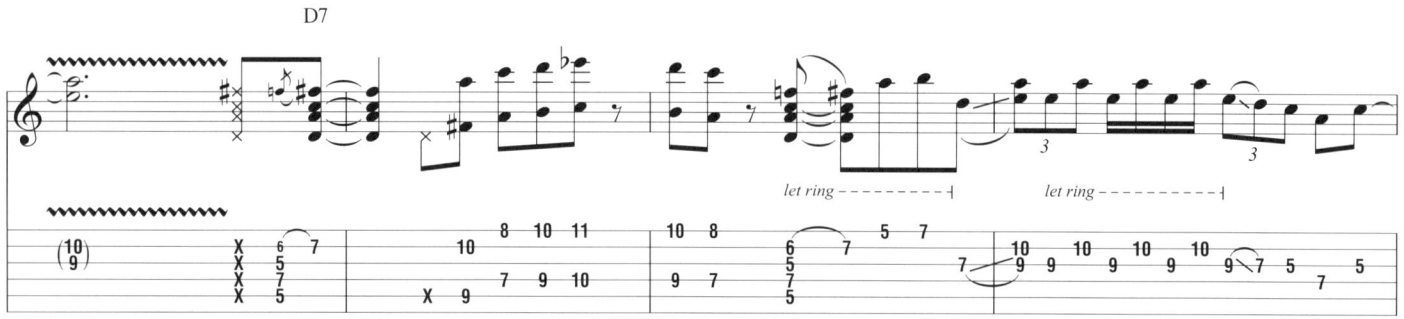

*T = Thumb on 6th string

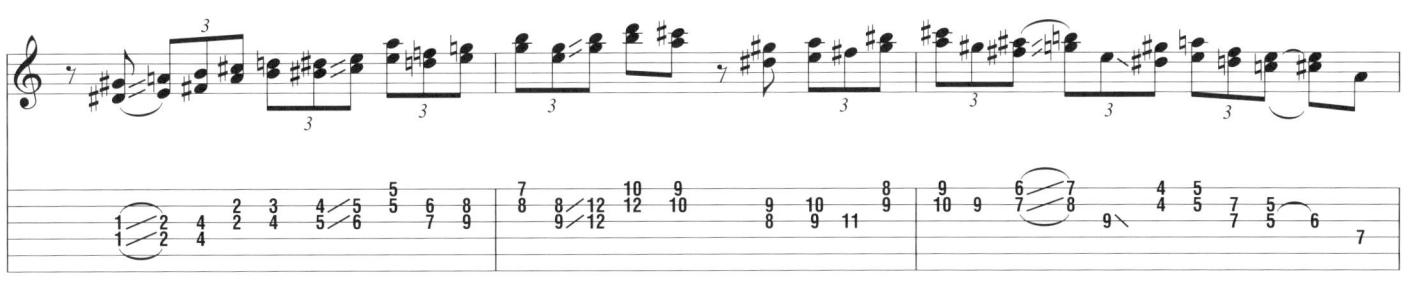

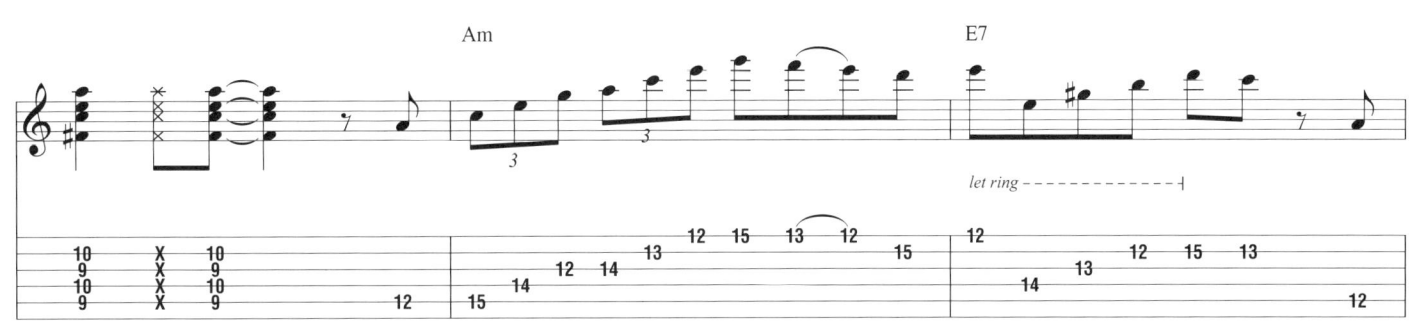

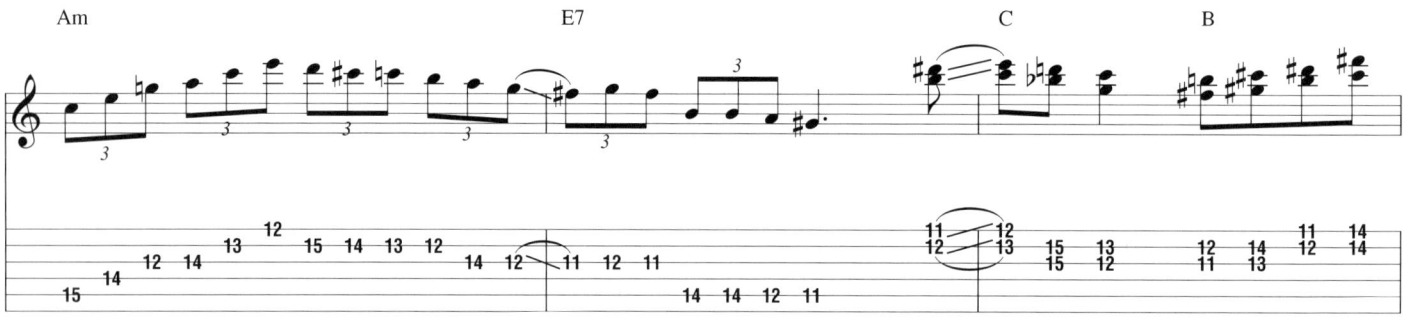

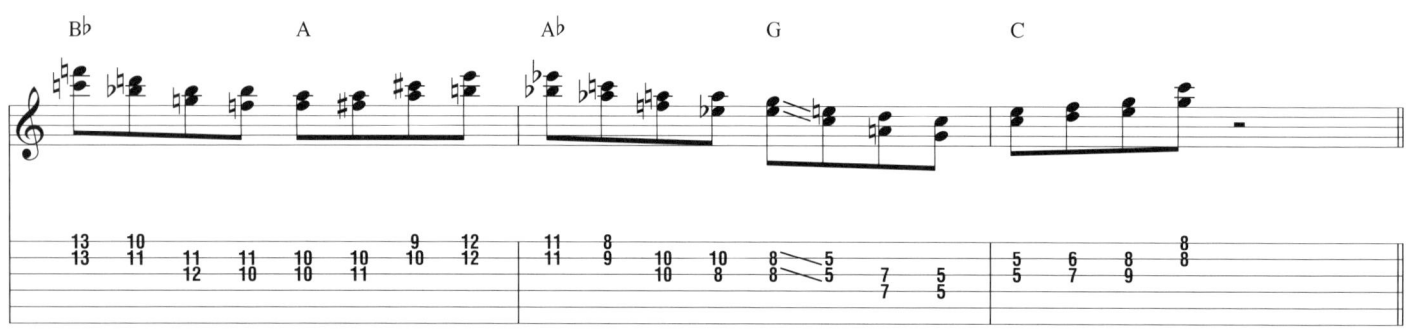

Example 80
(1:39)

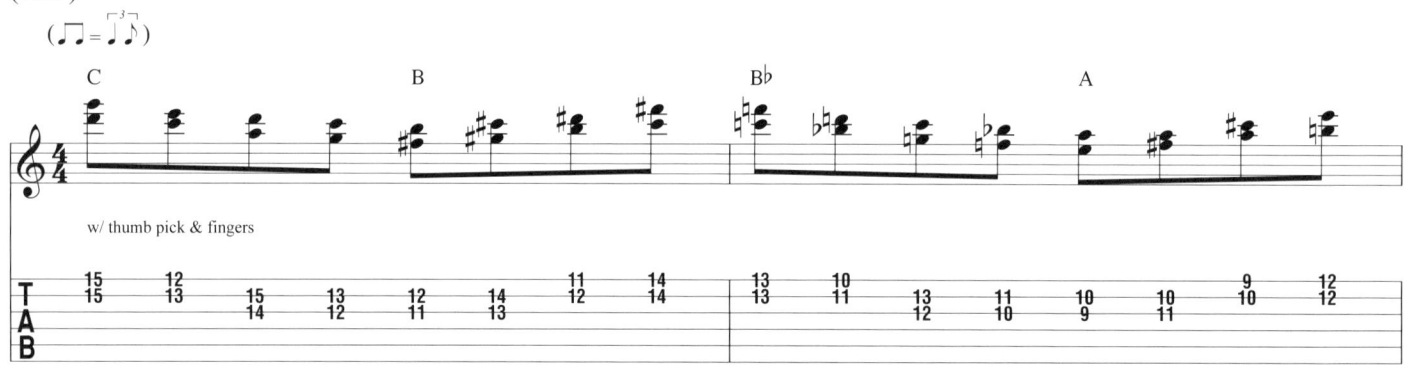

w/ thumb pick & fingers

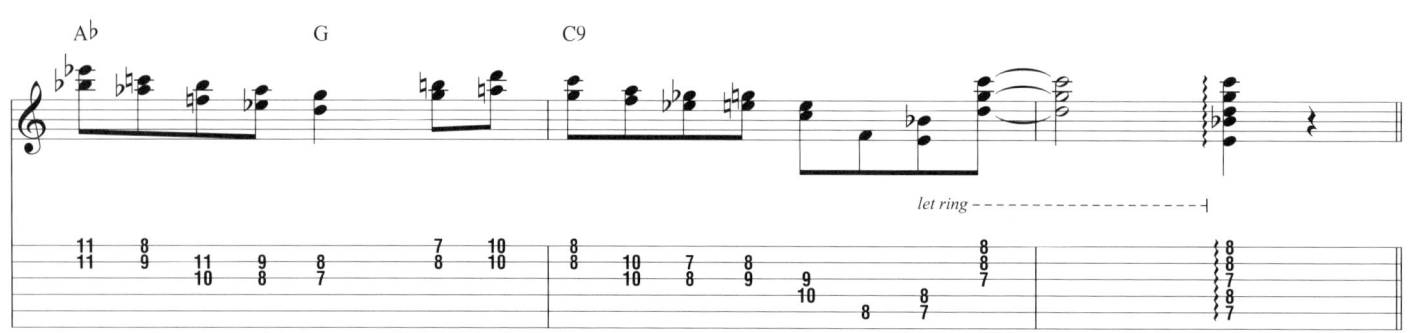

let ring

Chapter 12: Advanced Harmonization

Example 81
(:06)

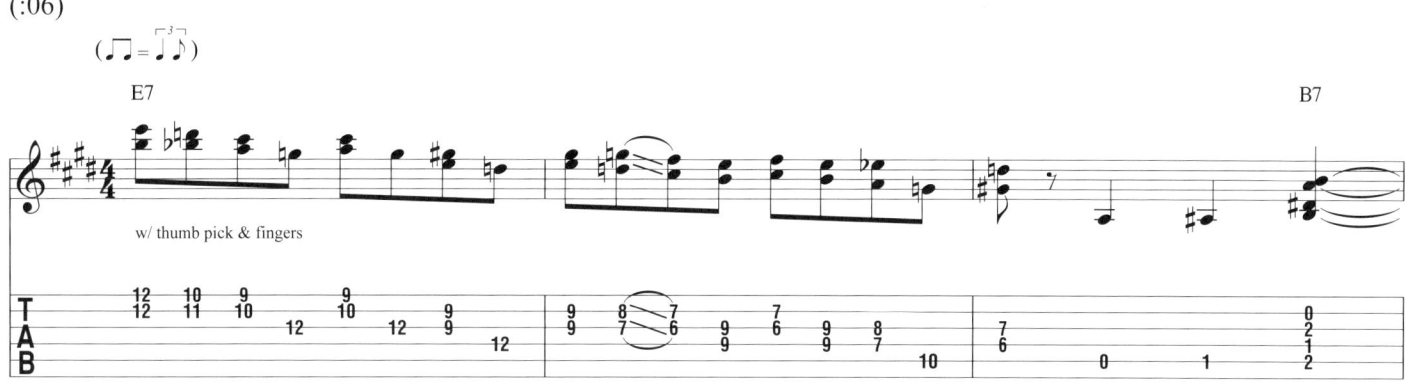

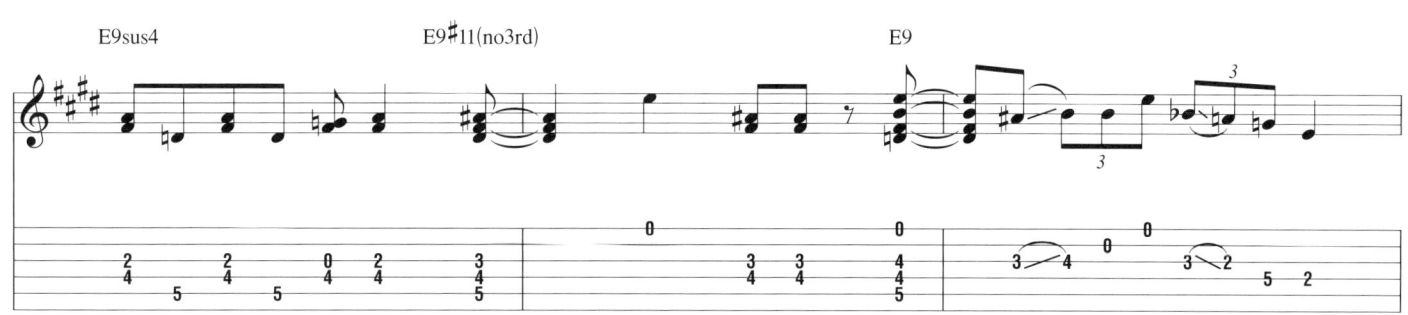

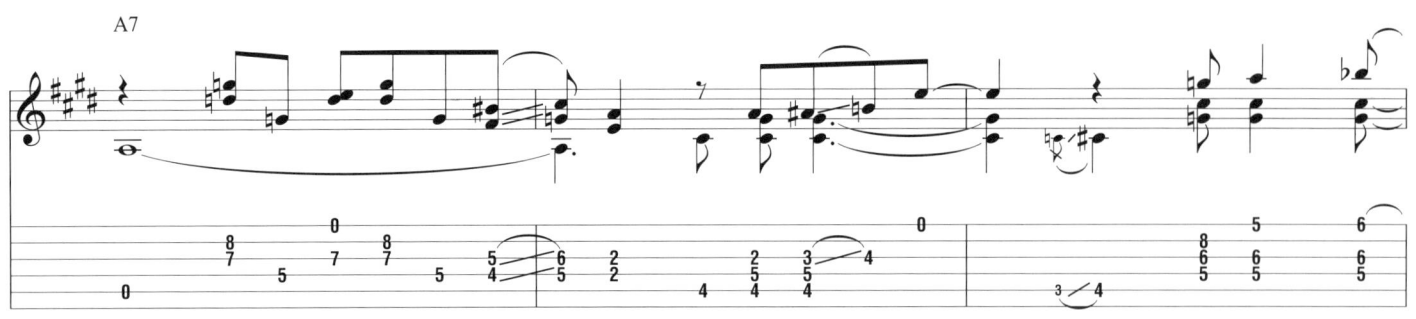
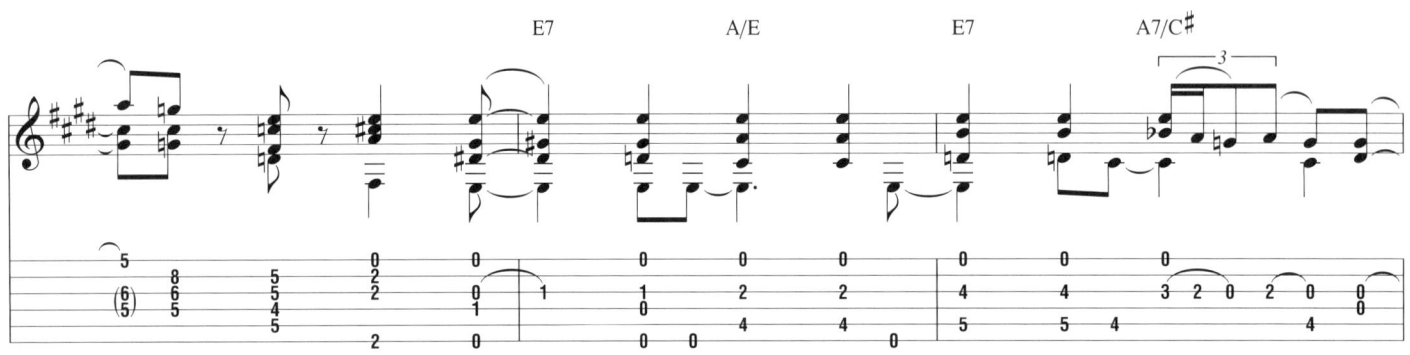
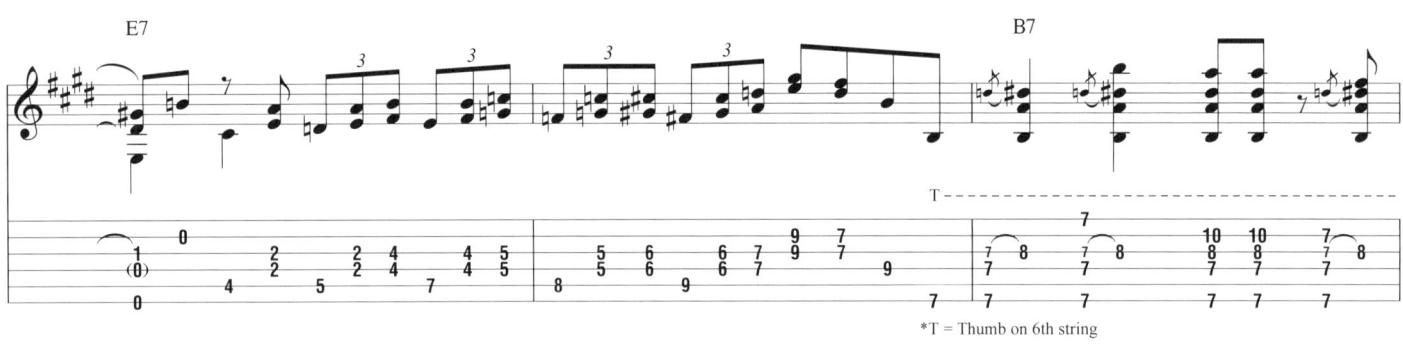

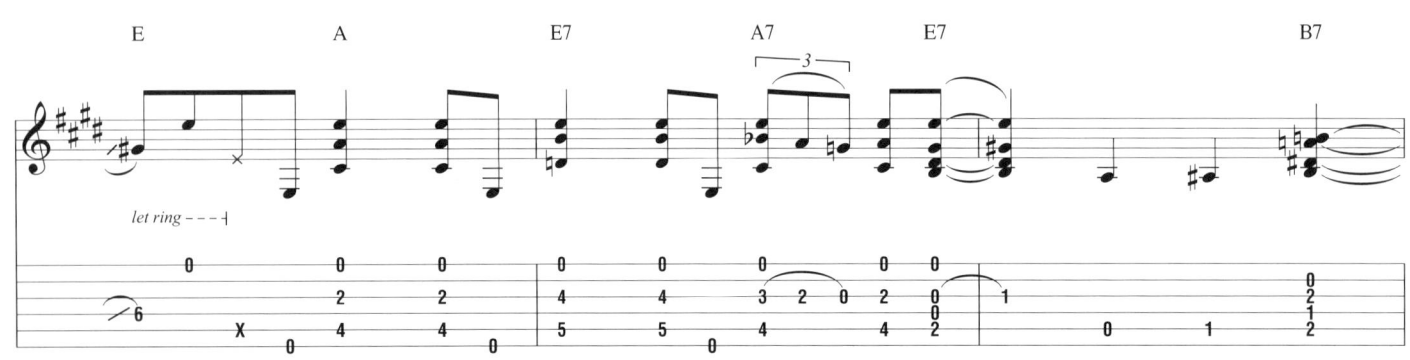

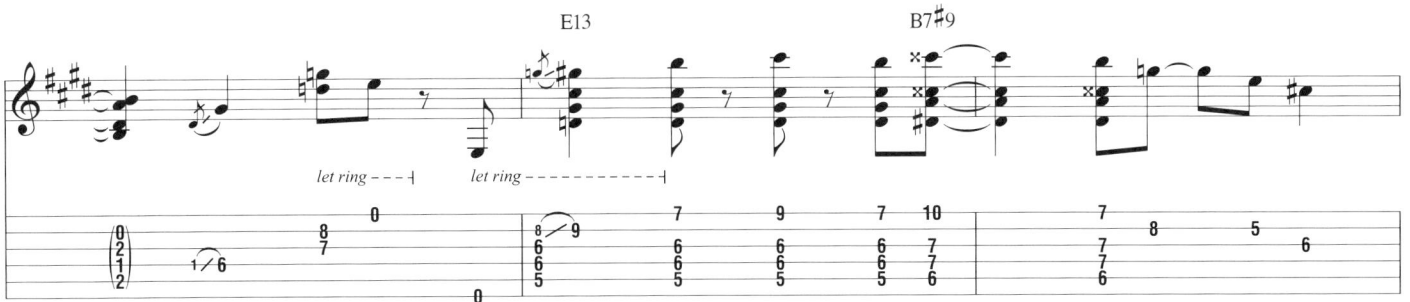

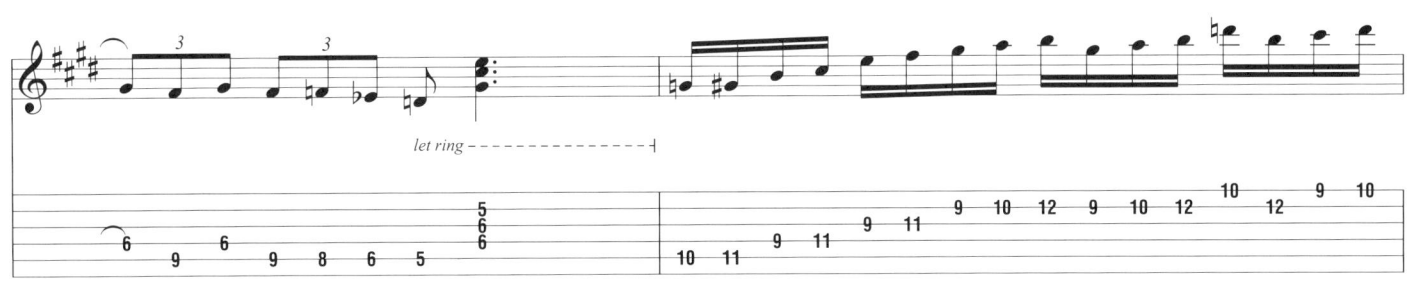
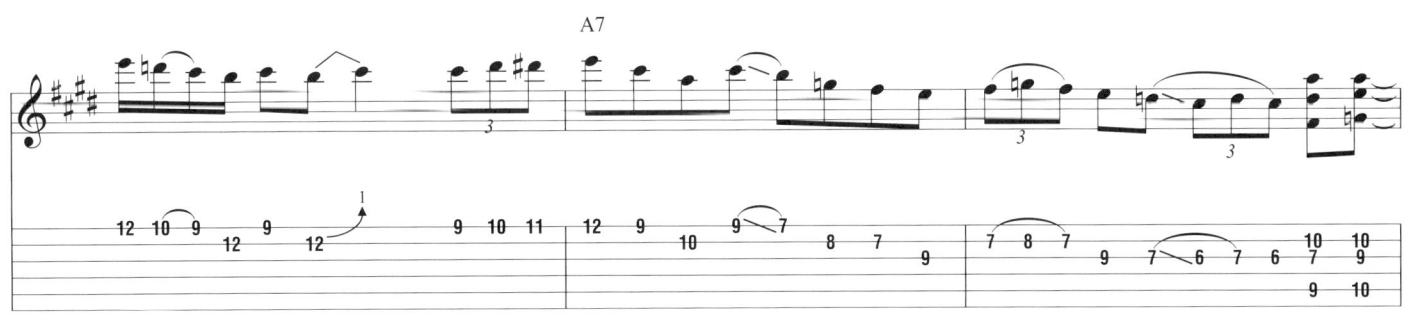
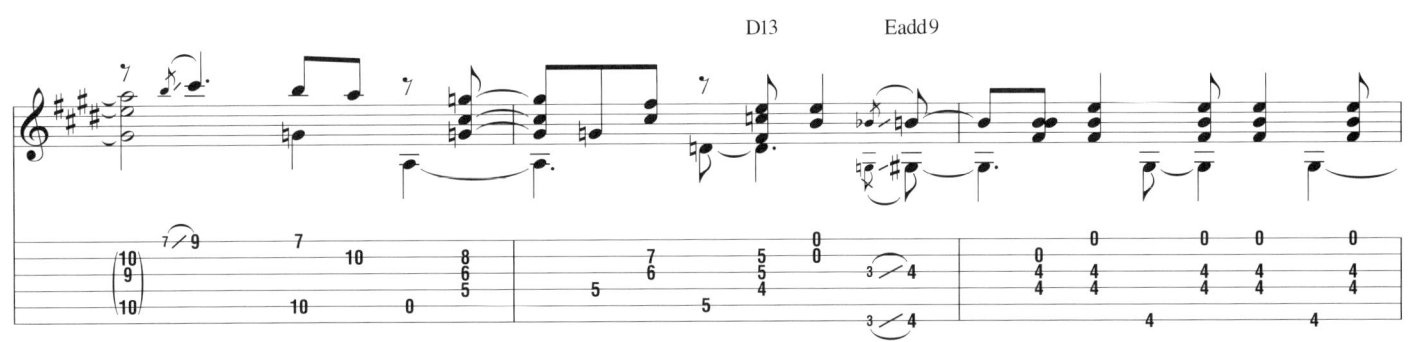

57

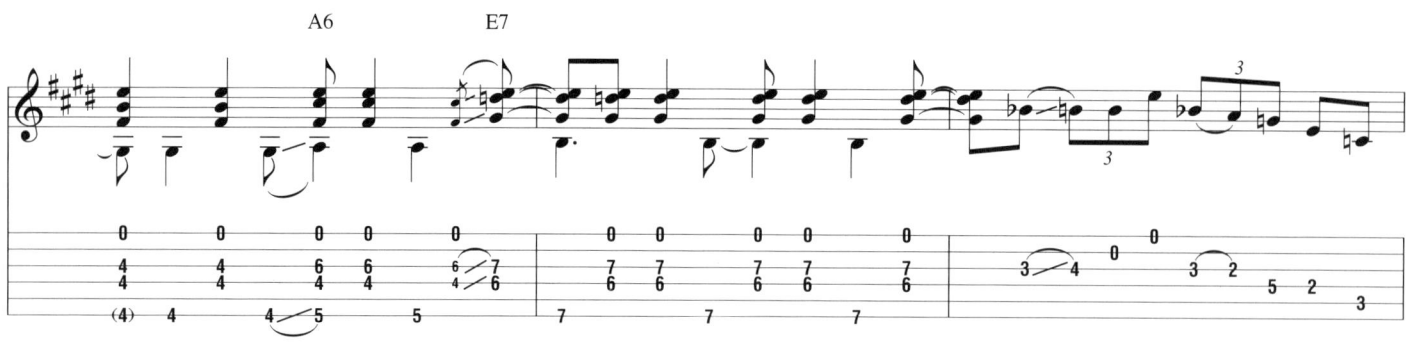
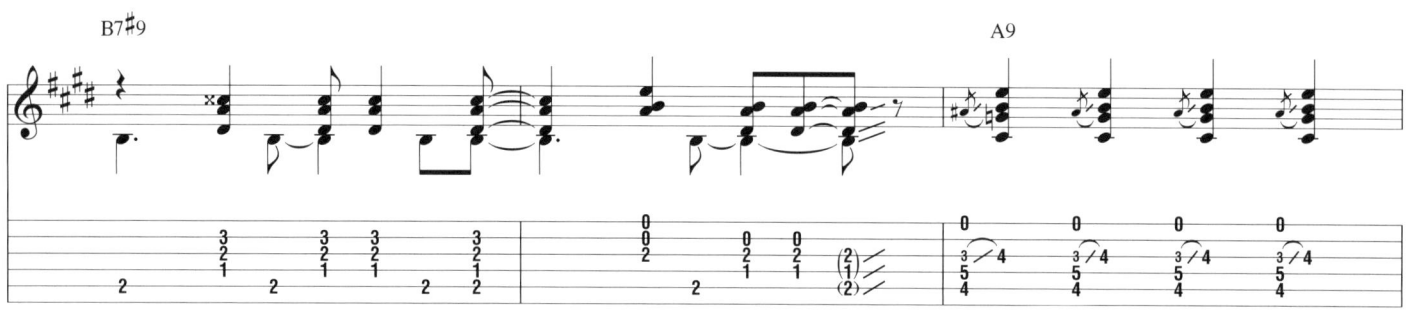
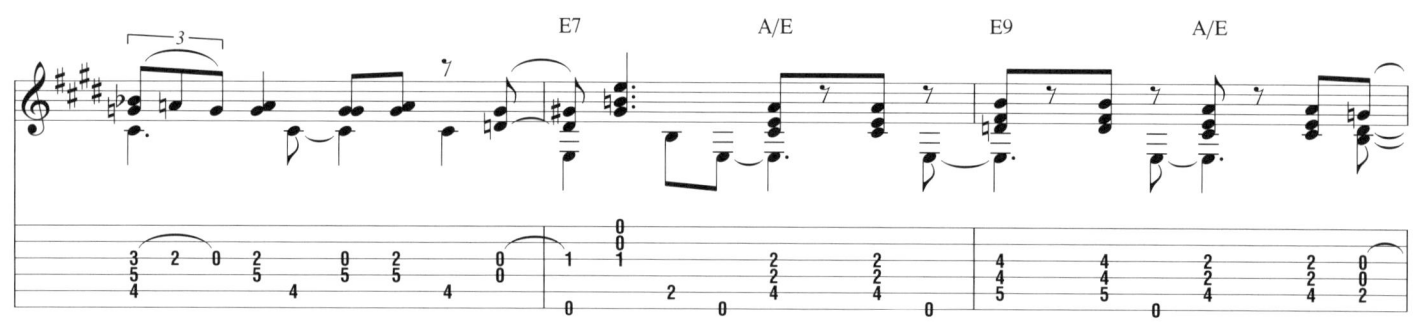

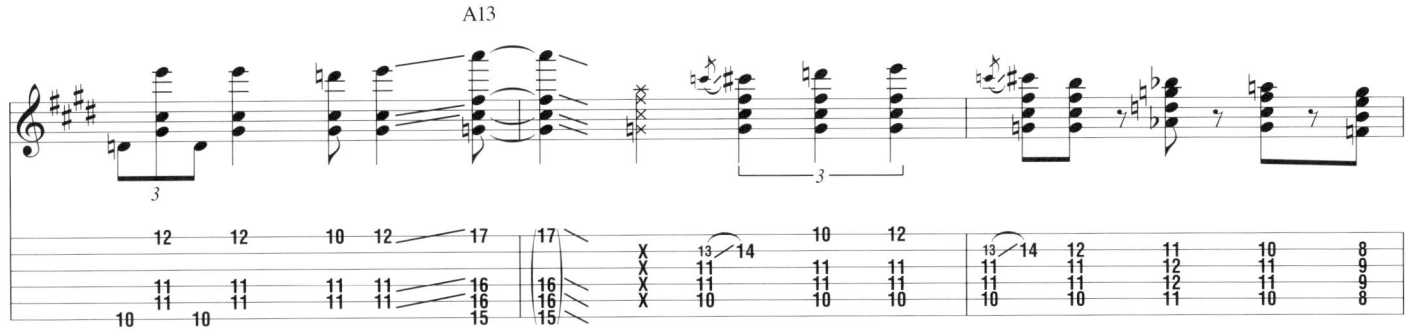
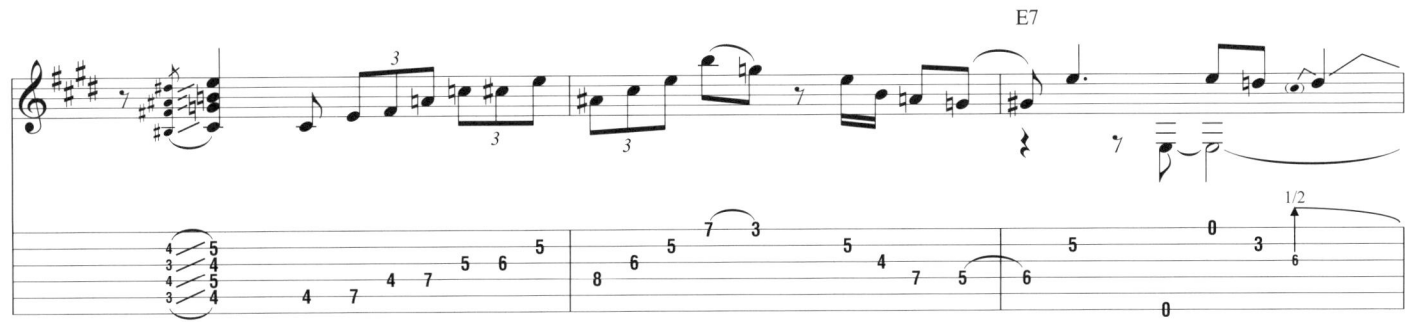

59

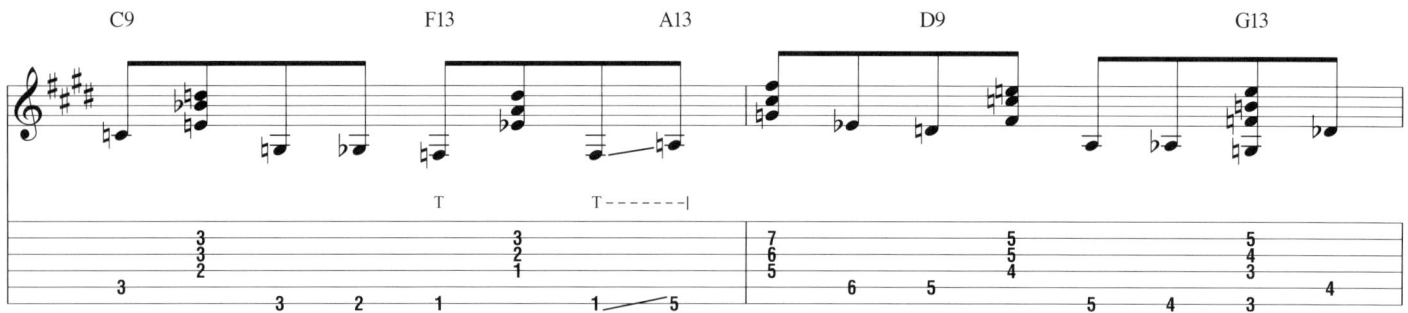

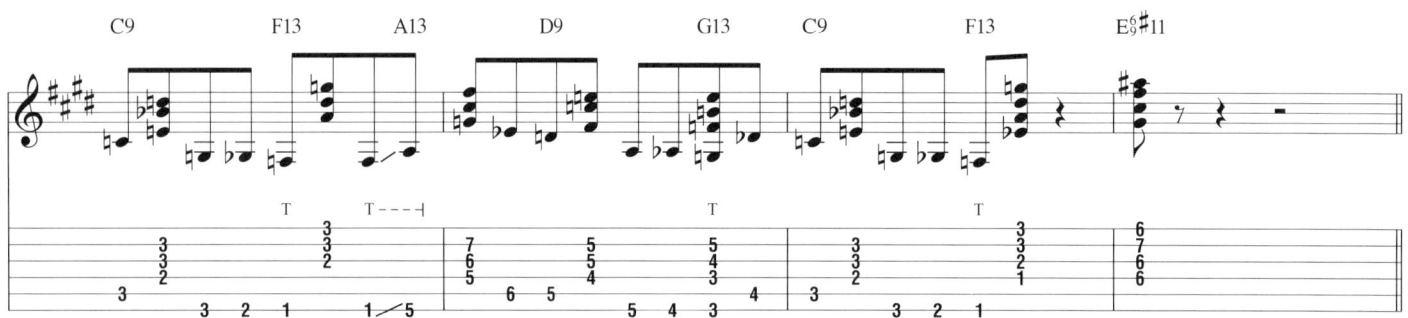

Example 82
(1:38)

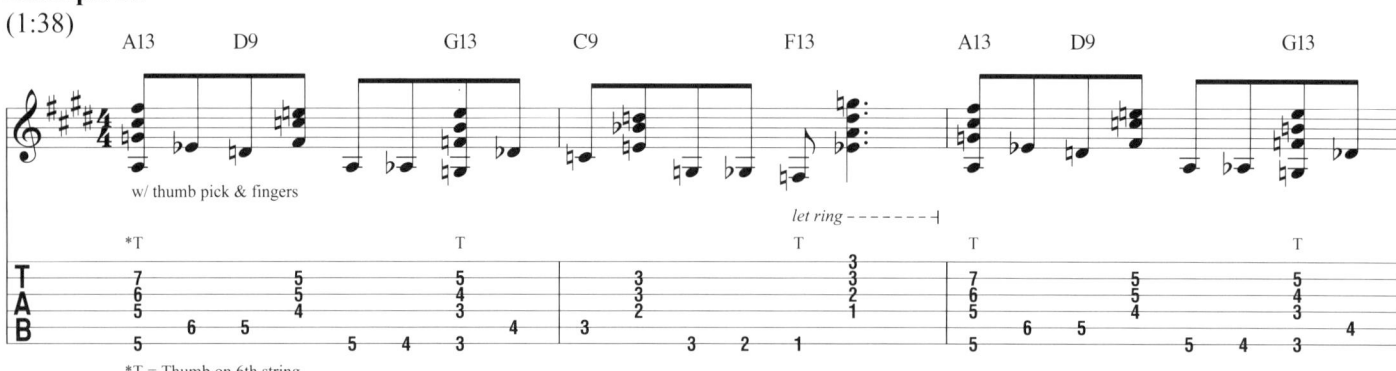

w/ thumb pick & fingers

*T = Thumb on 6th string

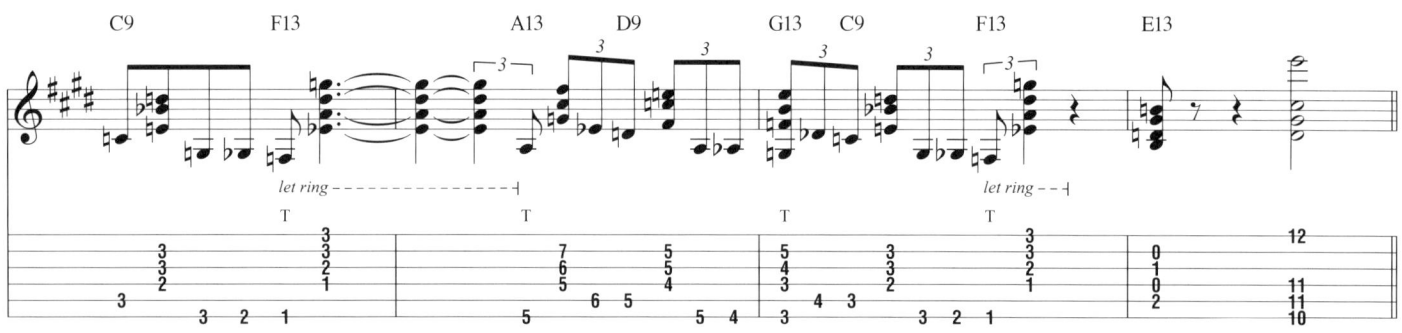

Chapter 13: Harp Harmonics

Example 83
(:06)

Example 84
(:22)

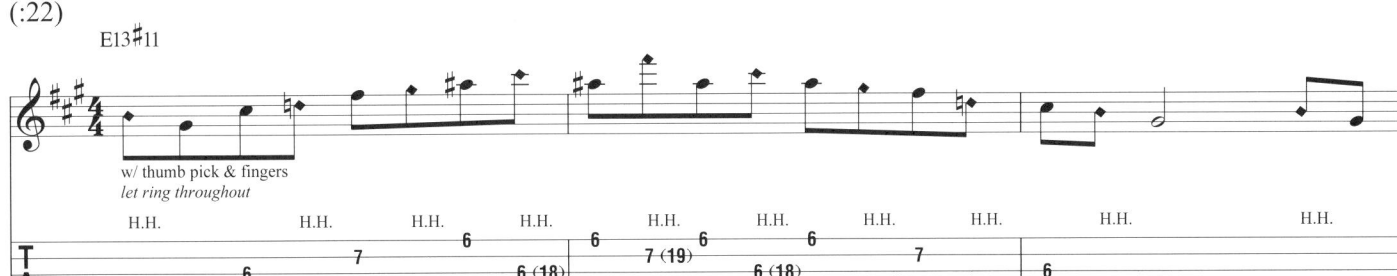

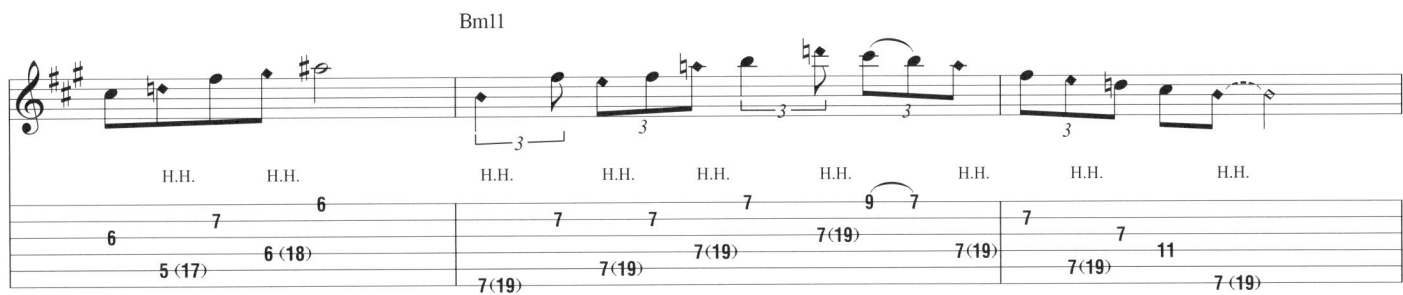

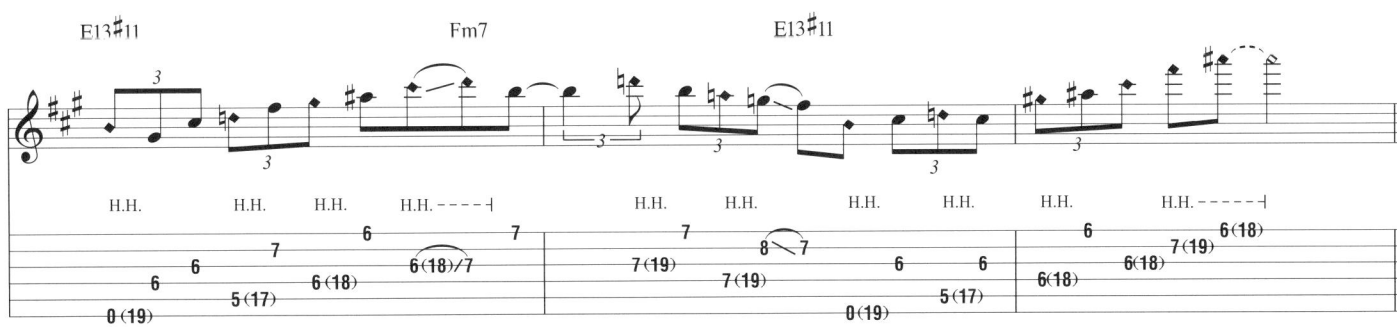

Example 85
(:36)

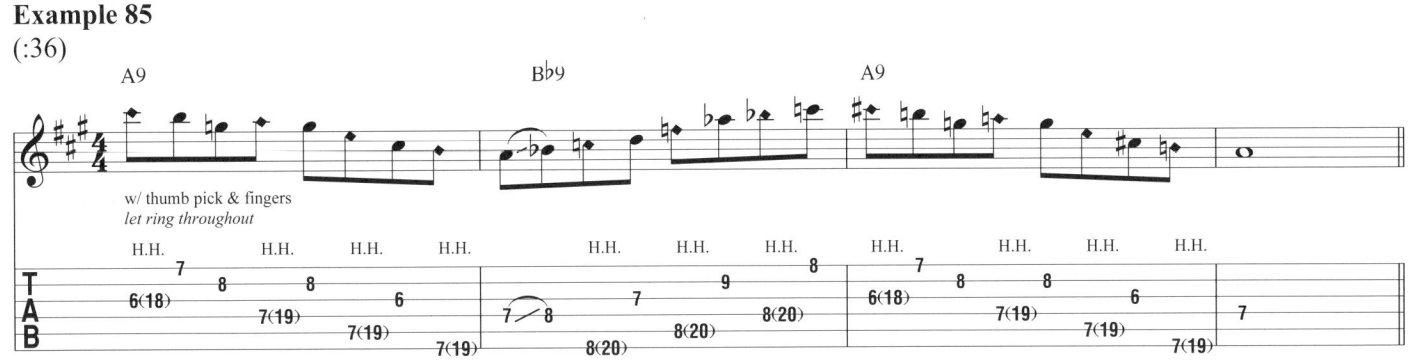

Example 86

(:42)

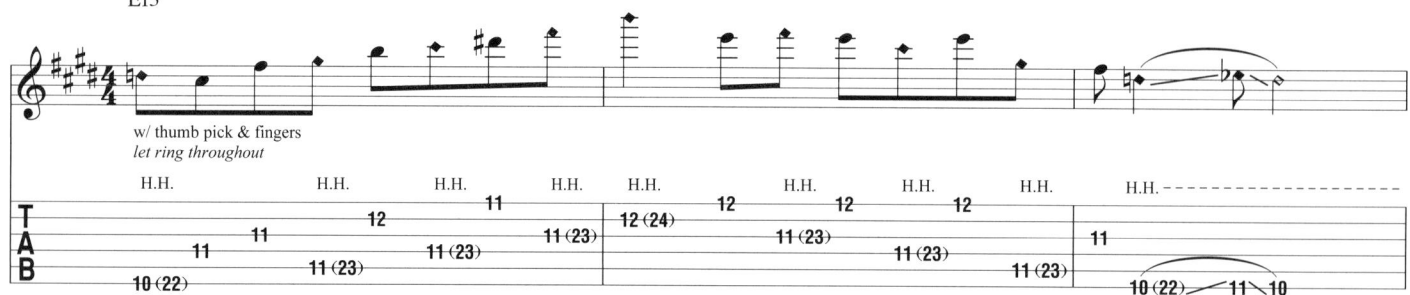

Example 87

(:50)

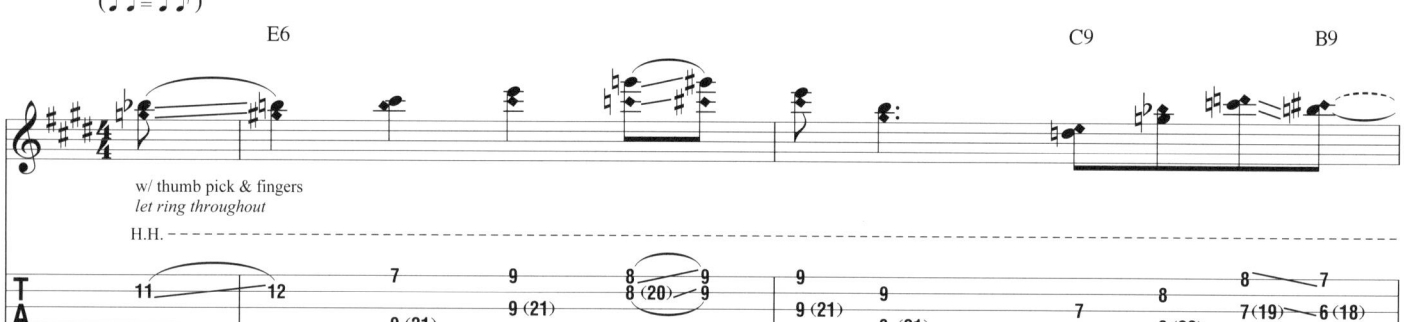

Example 88

(1:08)

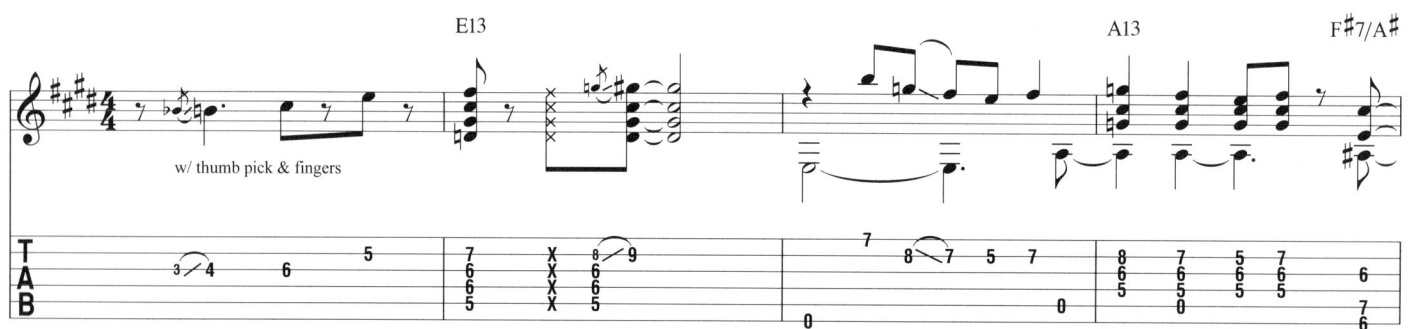

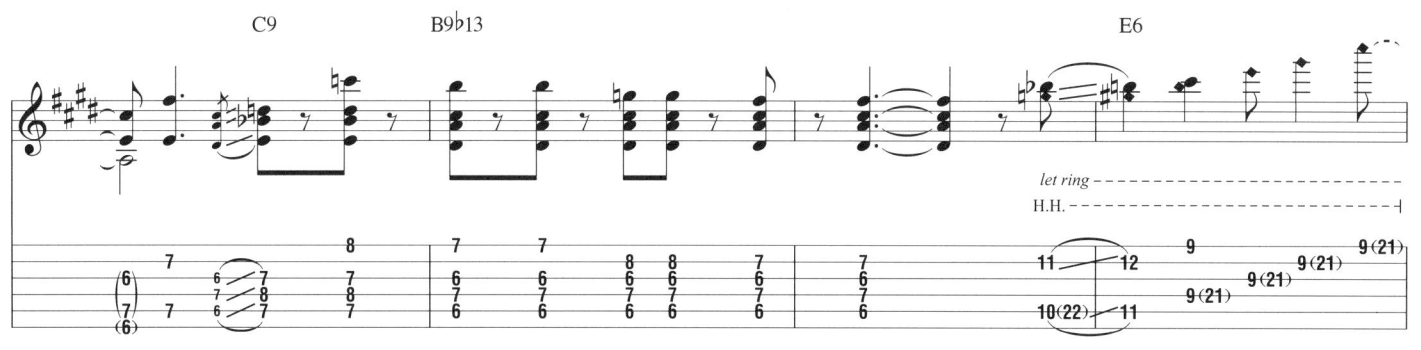
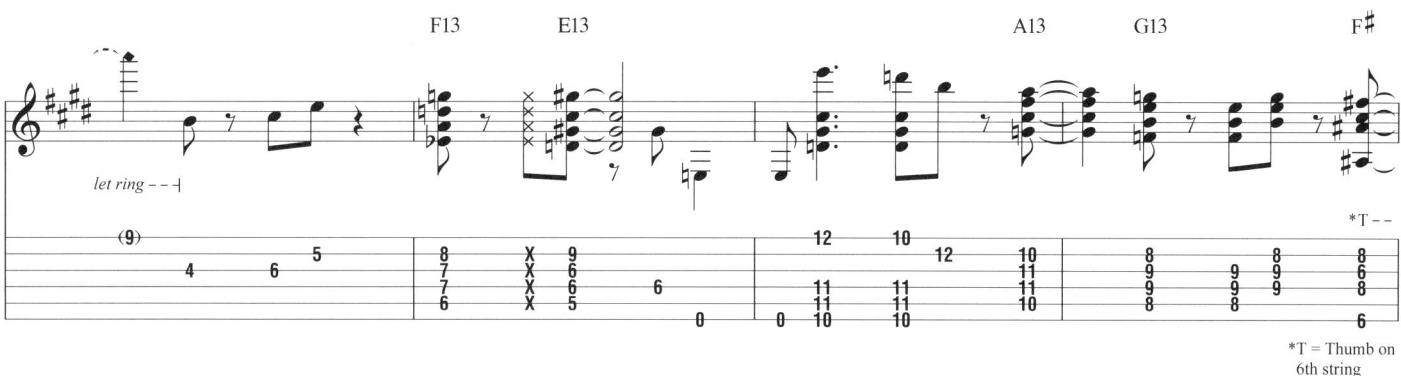

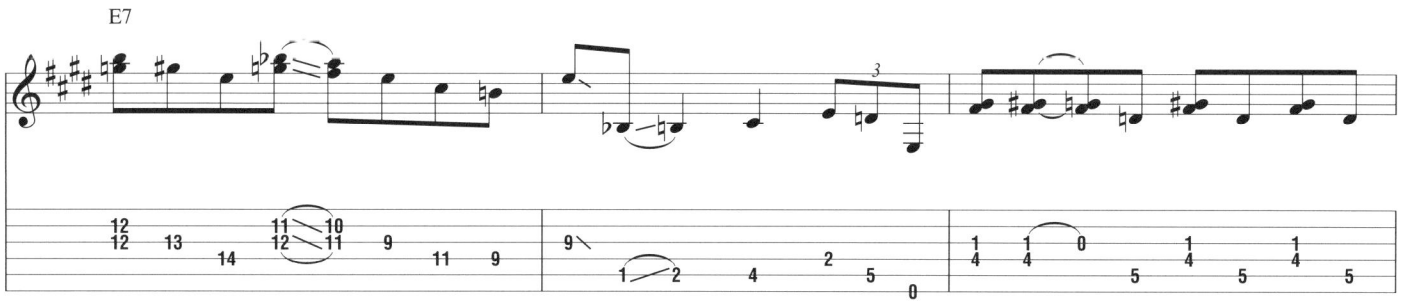
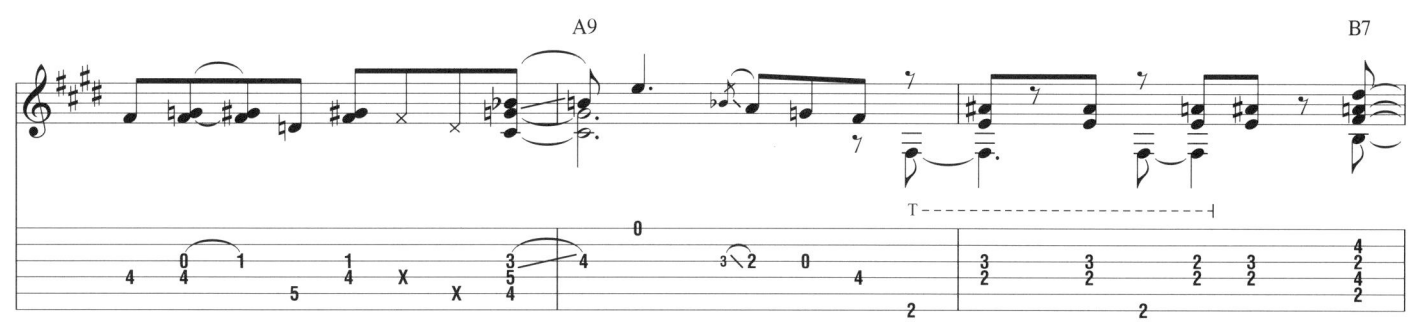

63

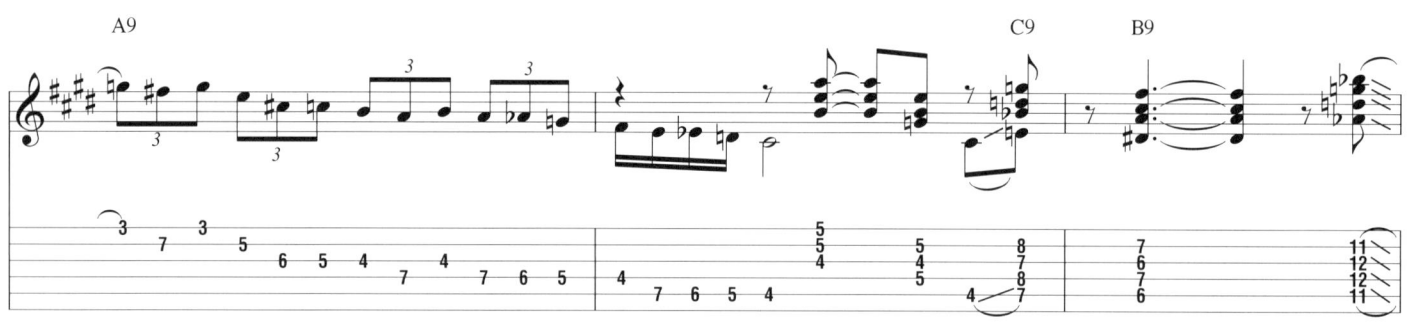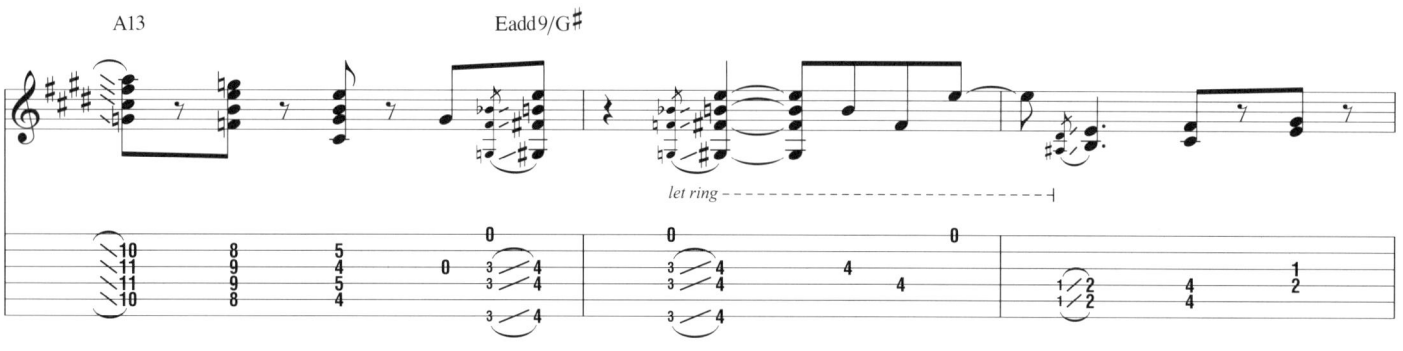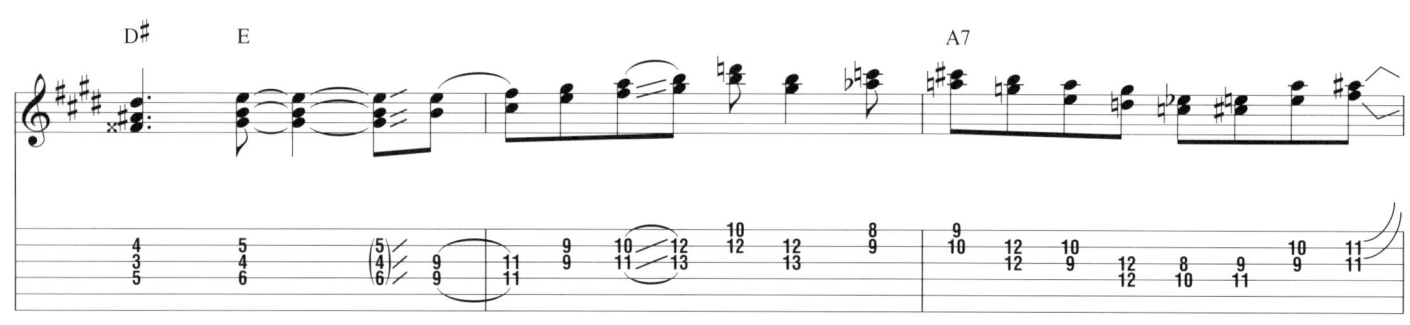

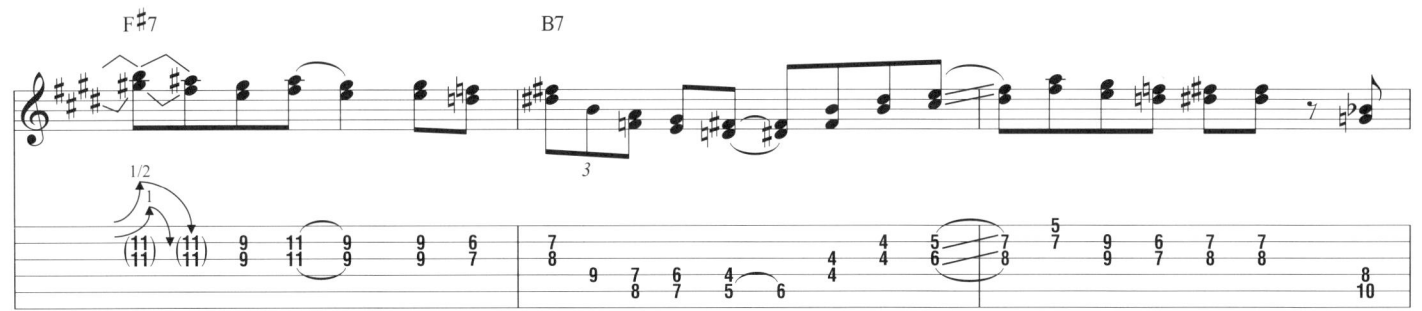
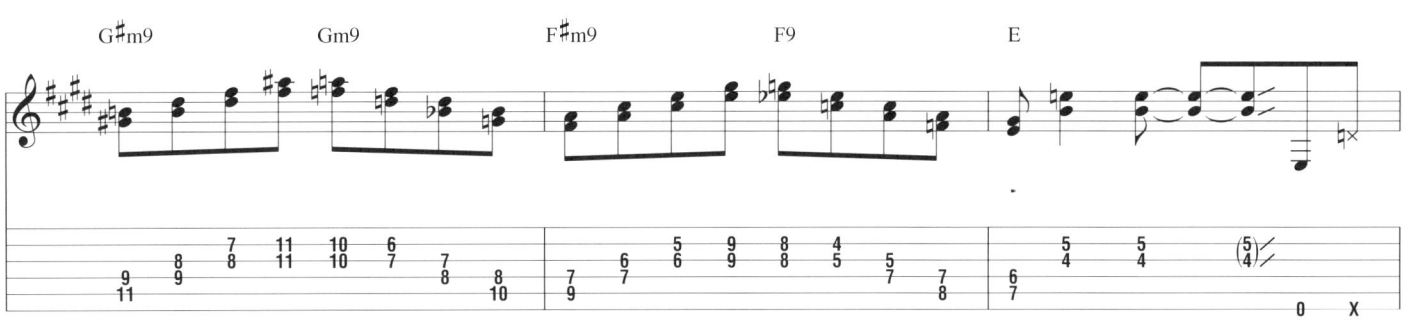
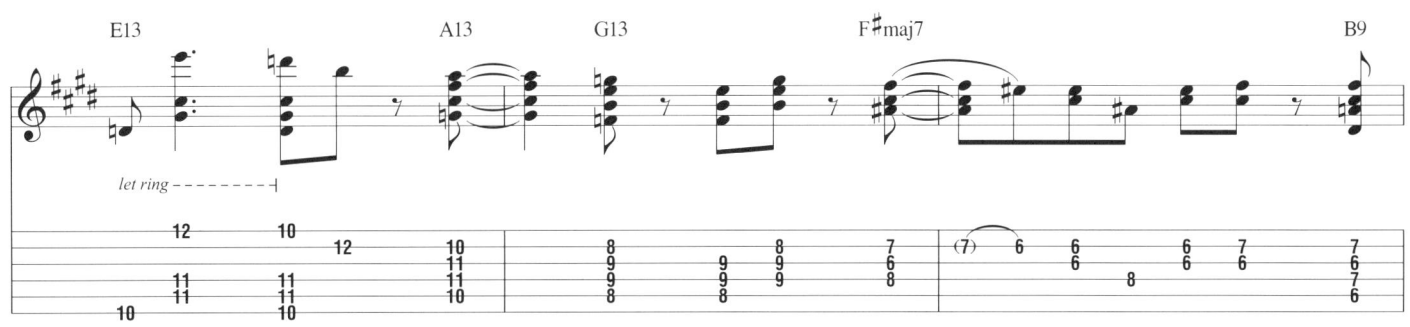

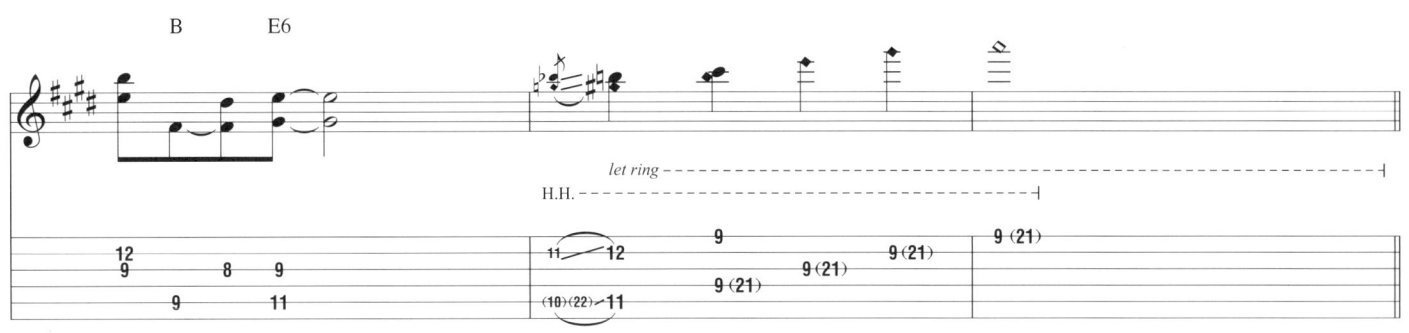

Chapter 14: Three-Note Chord Riffs and Licks in A

Example 89
(:09)

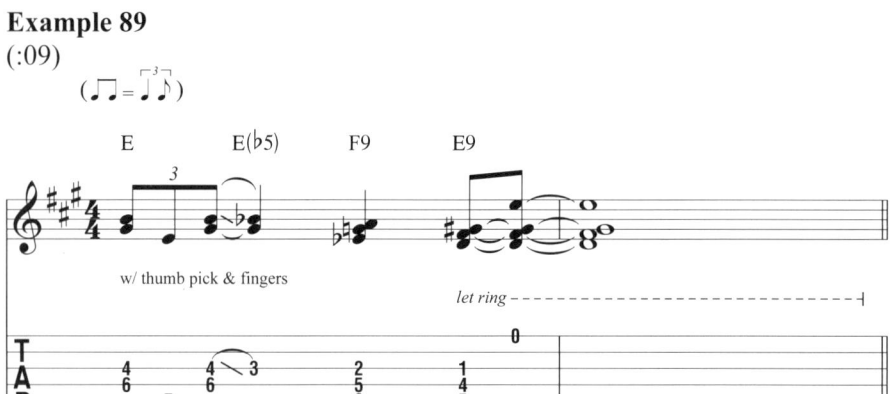

Example 90
(:43)

Example 91
(:47)

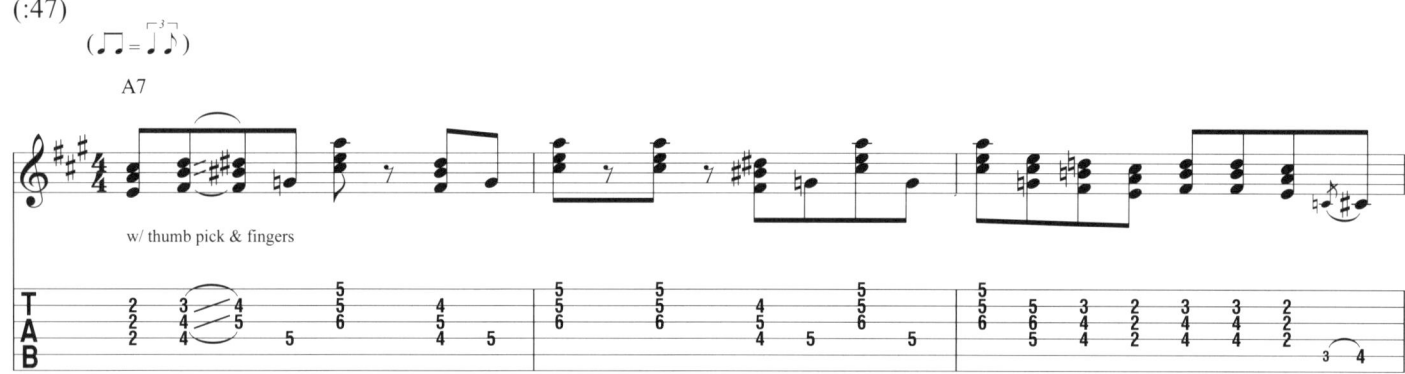

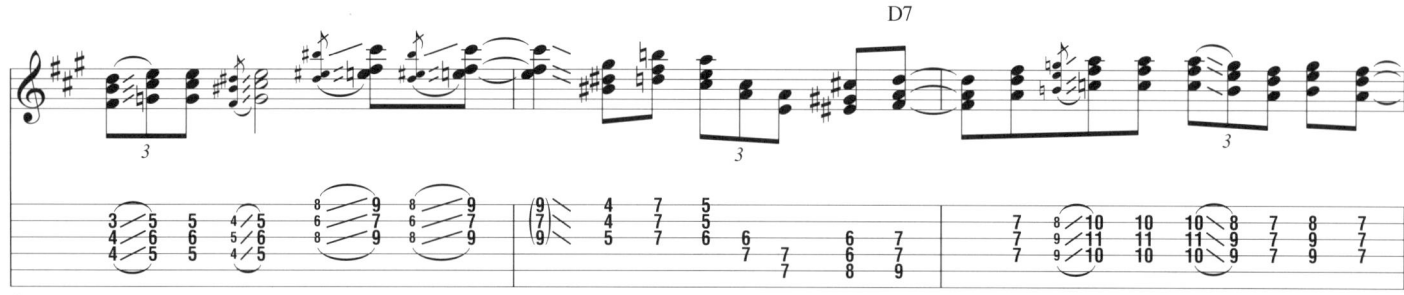

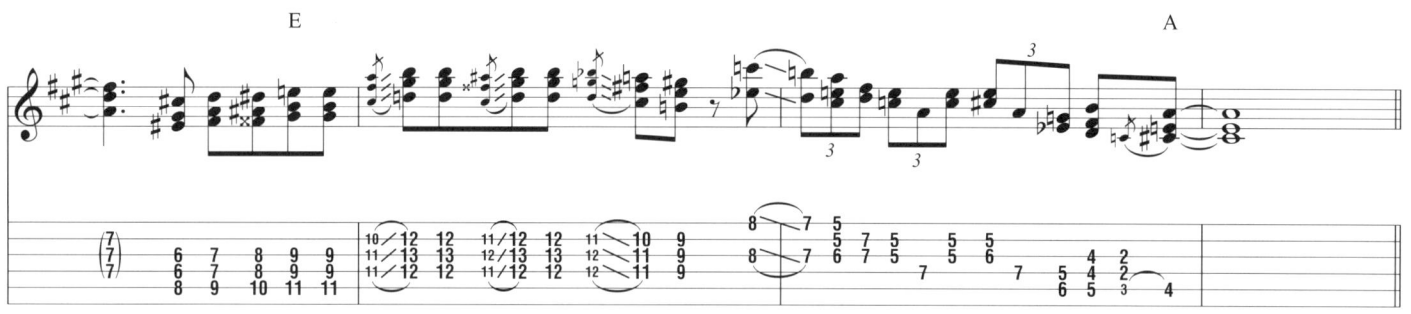

Example 92
(2:00)

Example 93
(2:11)

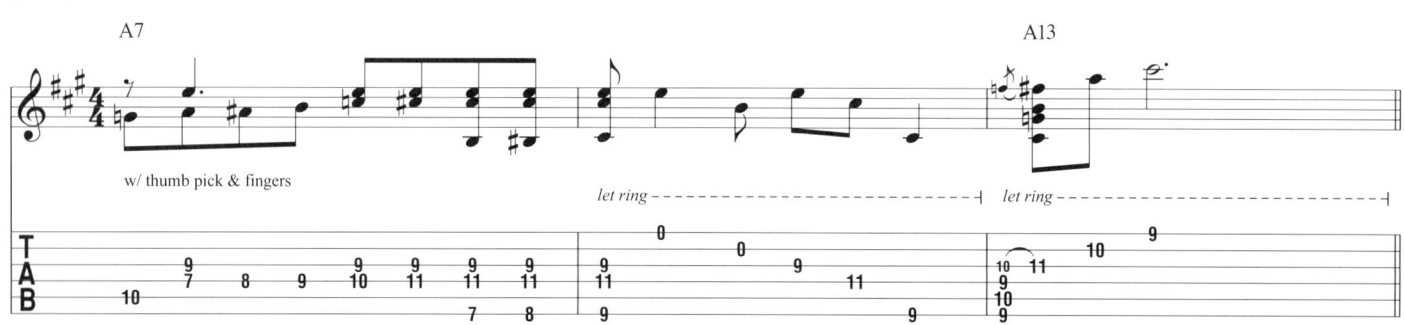

Example 94
(2:55)

Example 95
(3:03)

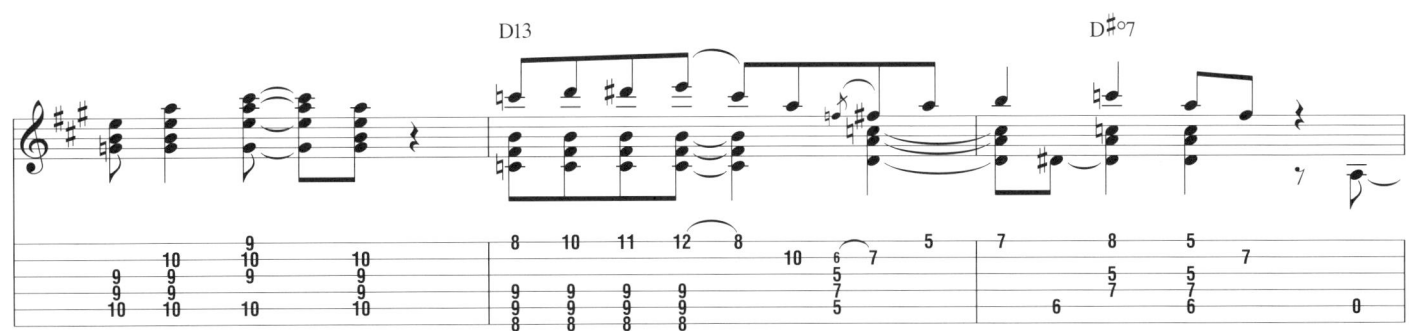

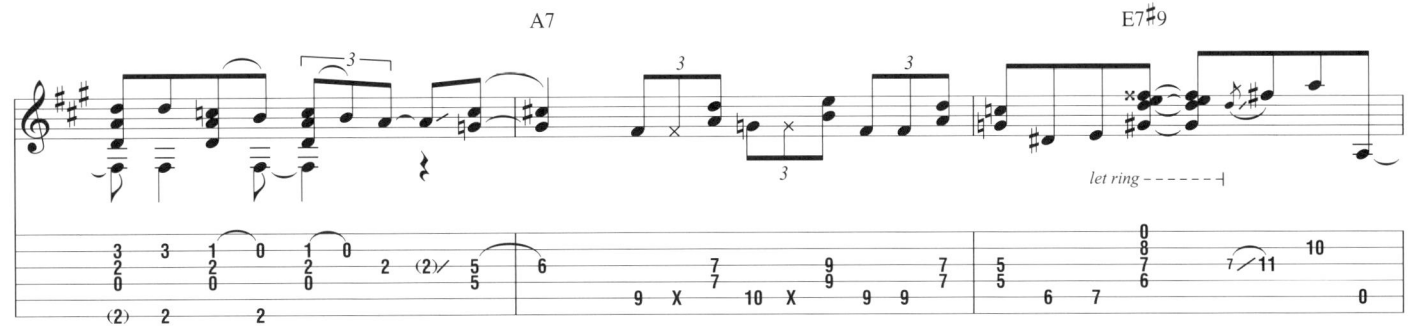

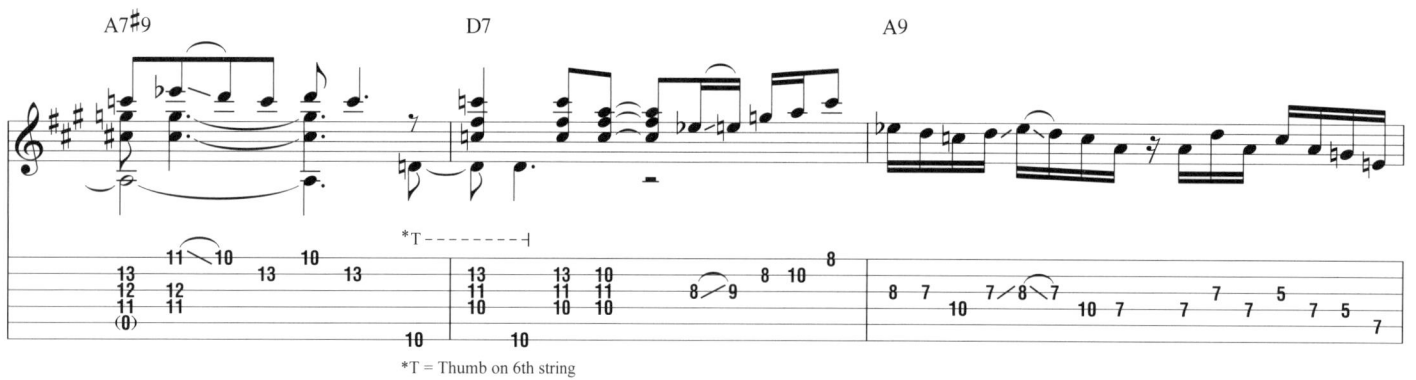
*T = Thumb on 6th string

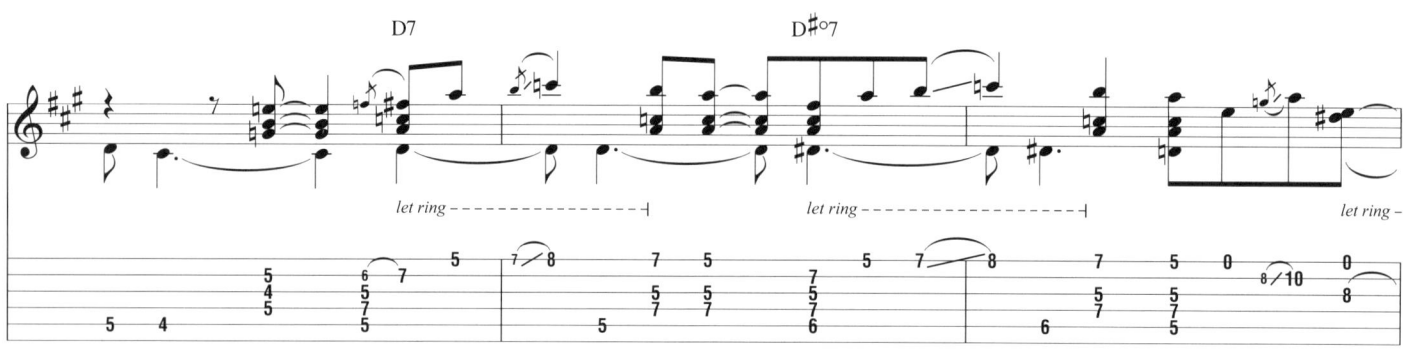

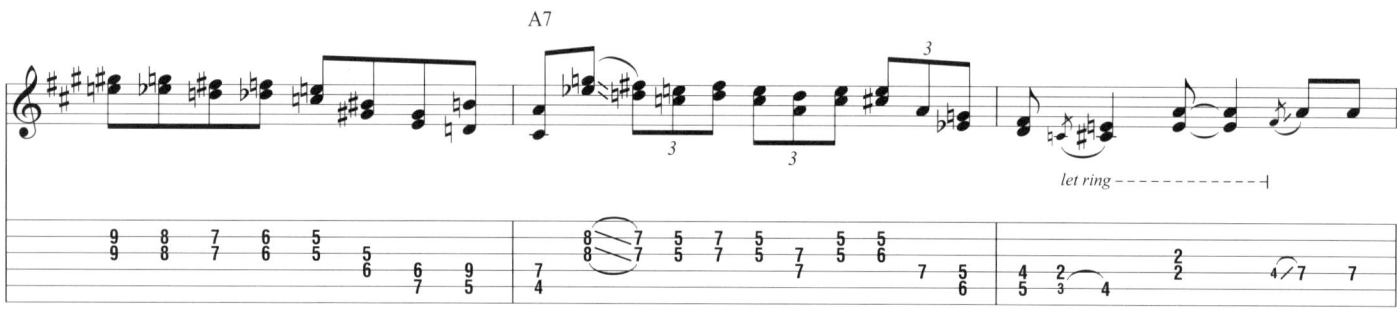

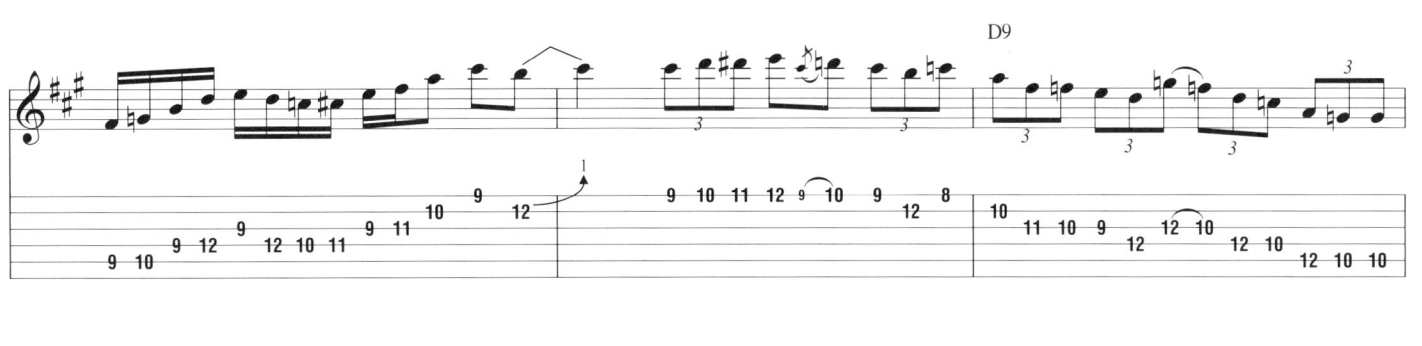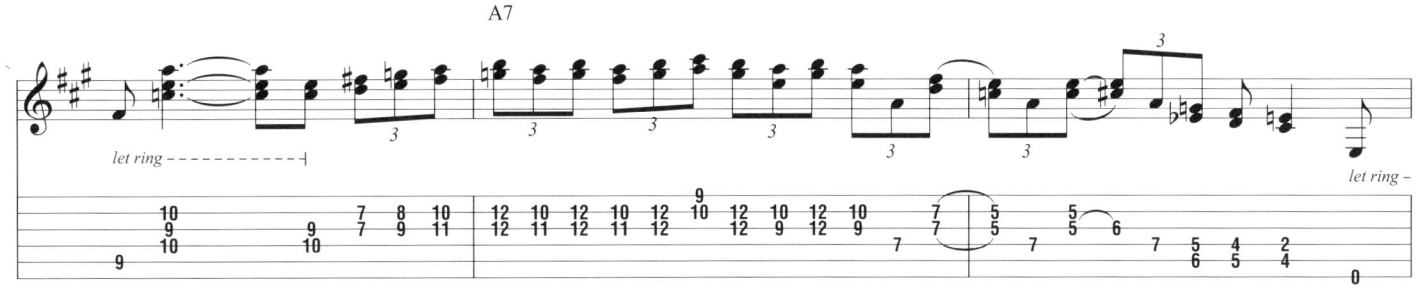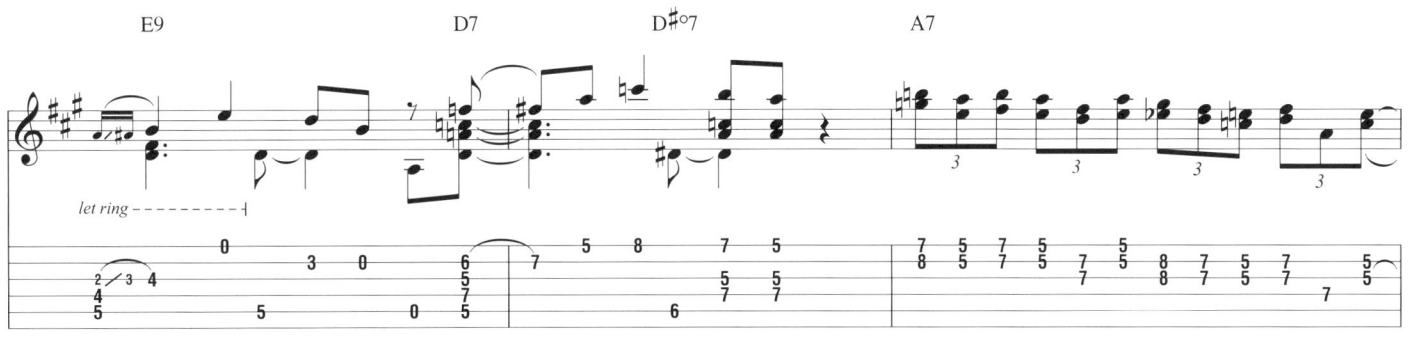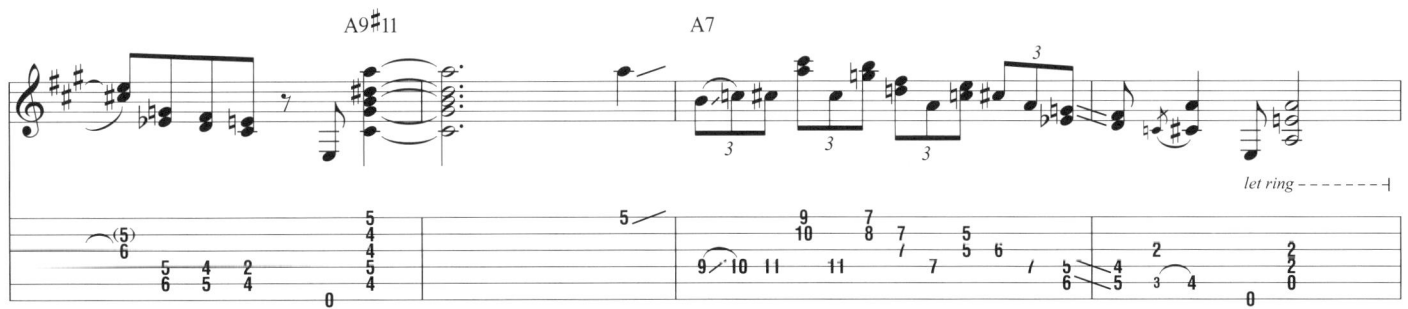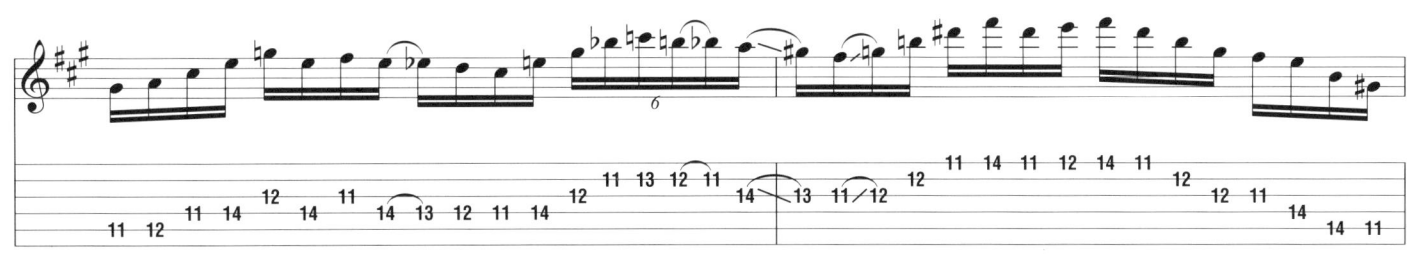

Chapter 15: Melodic Fingerstyle

Example 96
(:07)

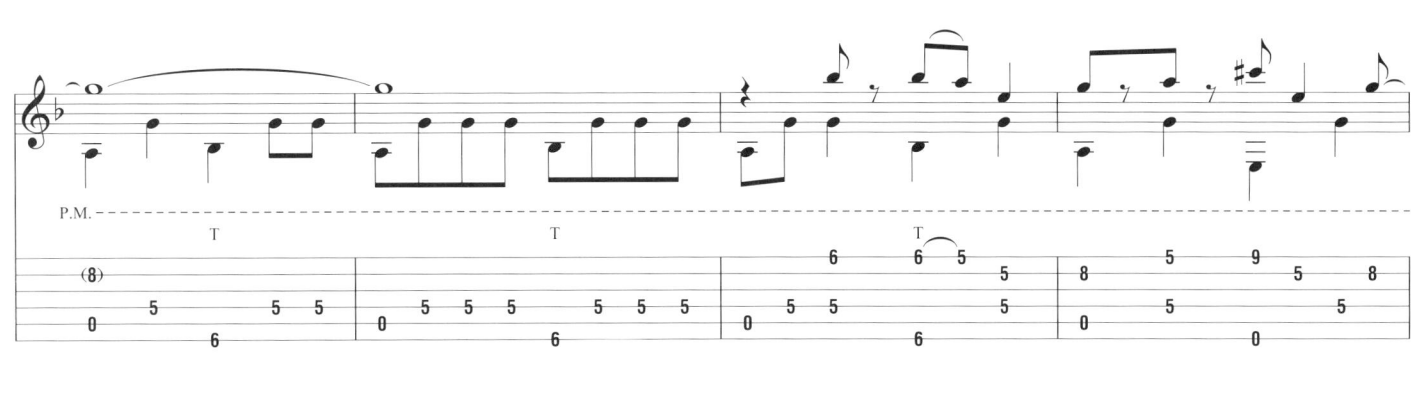
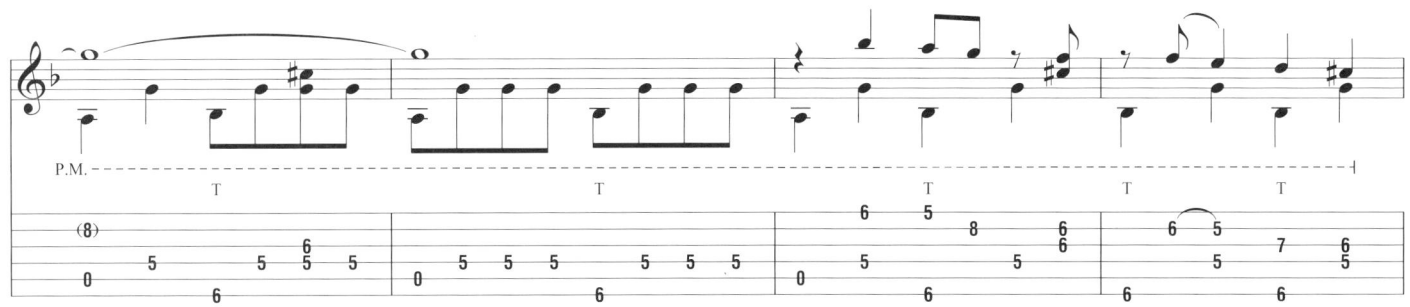
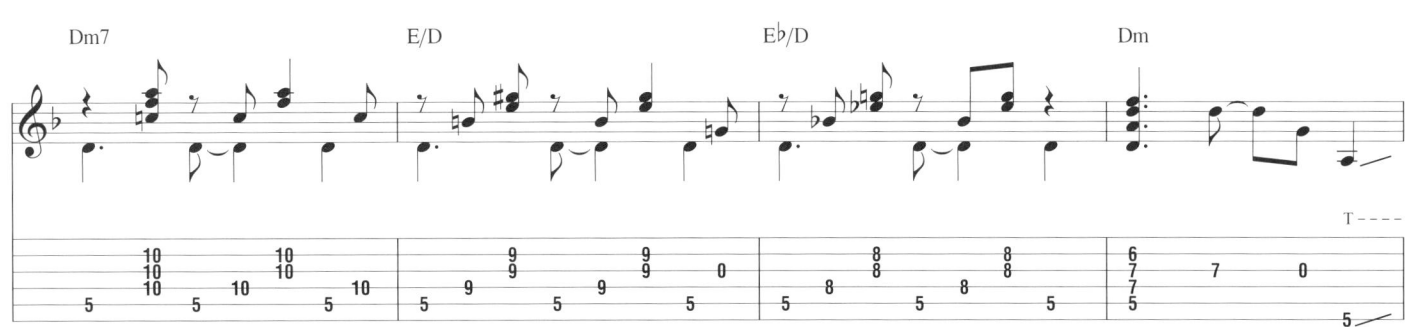

73

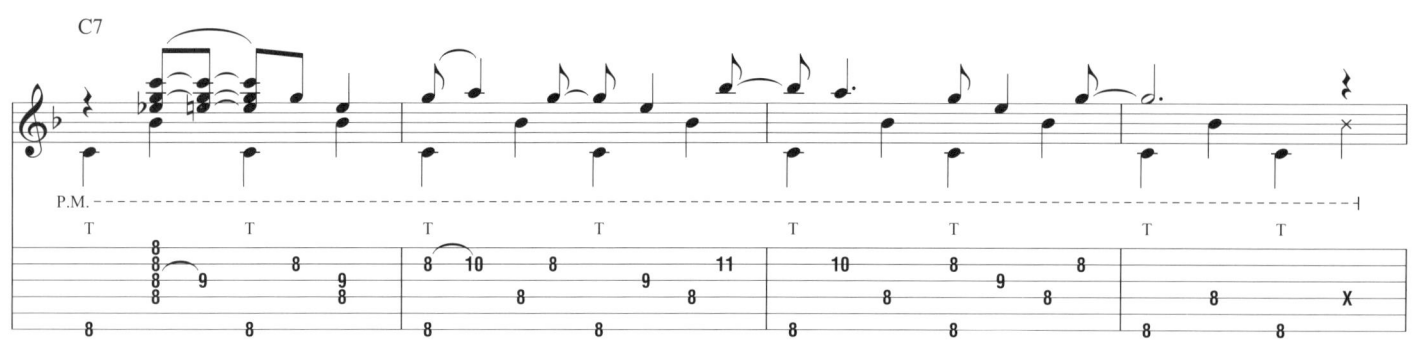

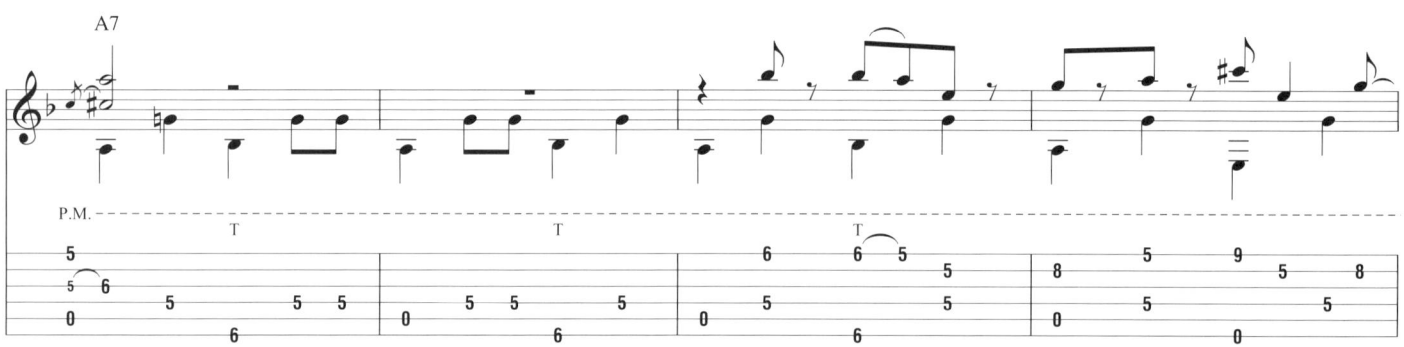
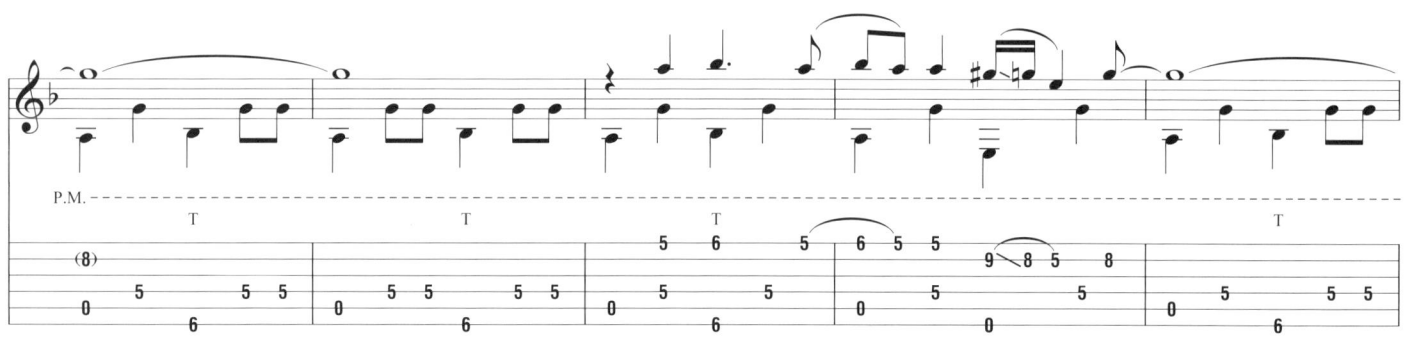

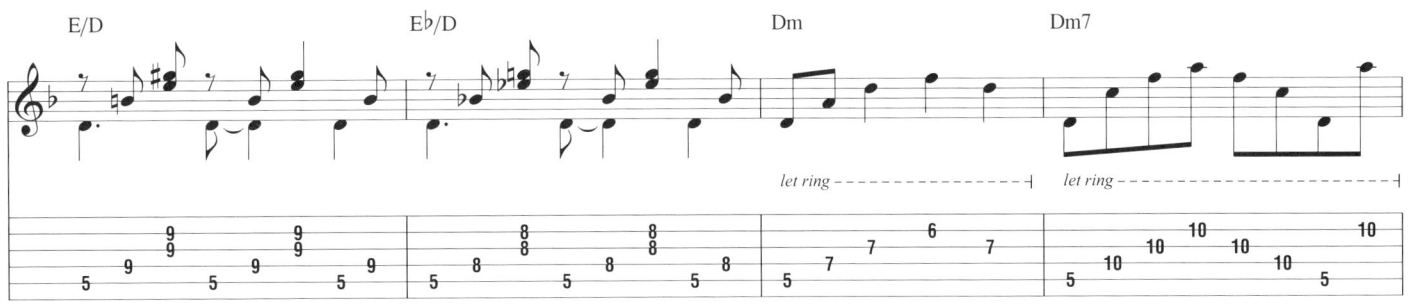

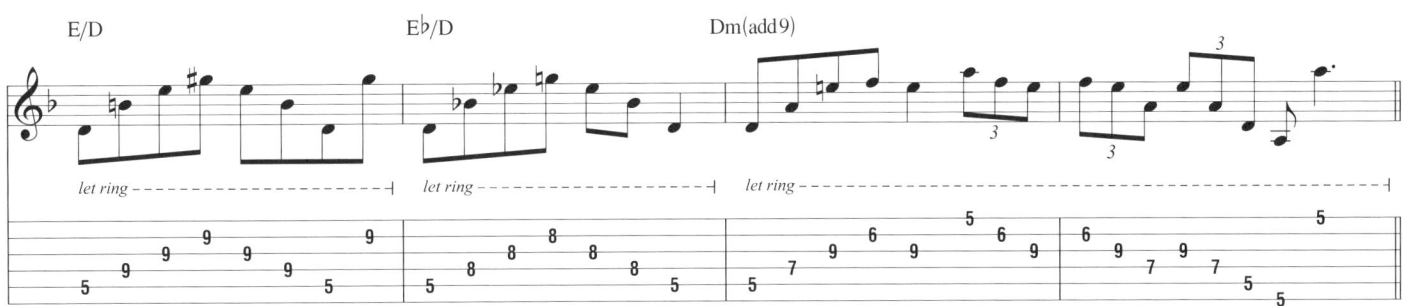

Example 97
(1:12)

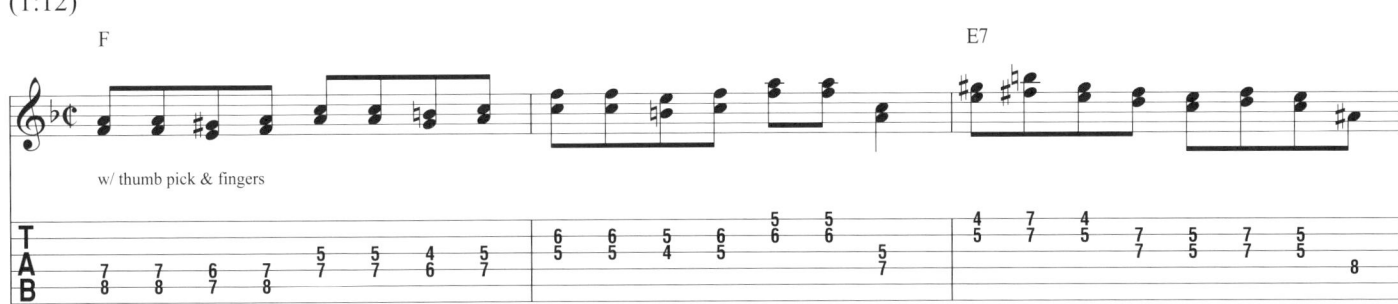

Example 98
(1:39)

GUITAR NOTATION LEGEND

Guitar music can be notated three different ways: on a *musical staff*, in *tablature*, and in *rhythm slashes*.

RHYTHM SLASHES are written above the staff. Strum chords in the rhythm indicated. Use the chord diagrams found at the top of the first page of the transcription for the appropriate chord voicings. Round noteheads indicate single notes.

THE MUSICAL STAFF shows pitches and rhythms and is divided by bar lines into measures. Pitches are named after the first seven letters of the alphabet.

TABLATURE graphically represents the guitar fingerboard. Each horizontal line represents a string, and each number represents a fret.

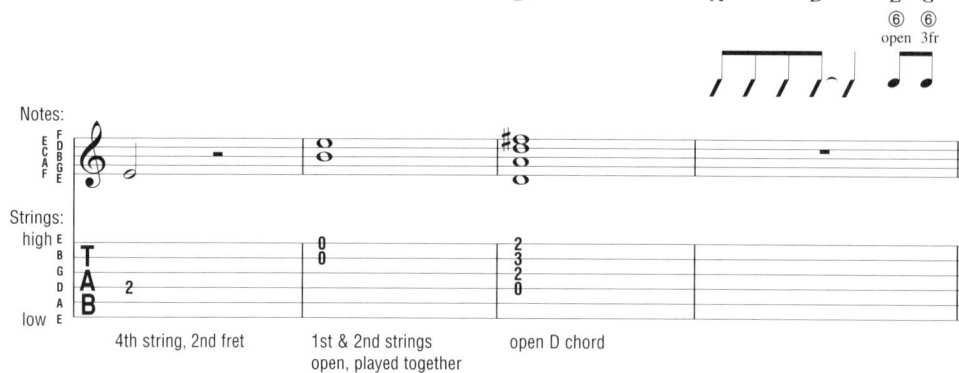

Definitions for Special Guitar Notation

HALF-STEP BEND: Strike the note and bend up 1/2 step.

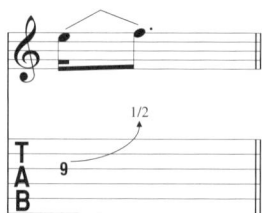

WHOLE-STEP BEND: Strike the note and bend up one step.

GRACE NOTE BEND: Strike the note and immediately bend up as indicated.

SLIGHT (MICROTONE) BEND: Strike the note and bend up 1/4 step.

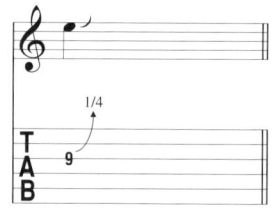

BEND AND RELEASE: Strike the note and bend up as indicated, then release back to the original note. Only the first note is struck.

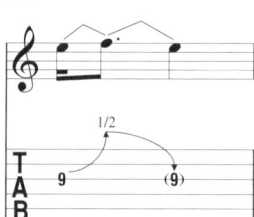

PRE-BEND: Bend the note as indicated, then strike it.

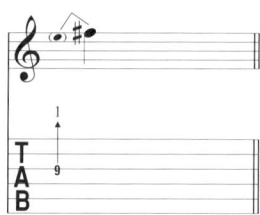

PRE-BEND AND RELEASE: Bend the note as indicated. Strike it and release the bend back to the original note.

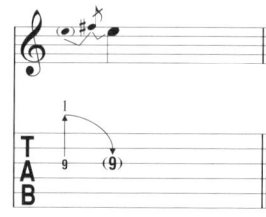

UNISON BEND: Strike the two notes simultaneously and bend the lower note up to the pitch of the higher.

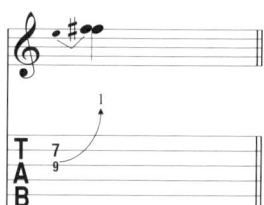

VIBRATO: The string is vibrated by rapidly bending and releasing the note with the fretting hand.

WIDE VIBRATO: The pitch is varied to a greater degree by vibrating with the fretting hand.

HAMMER-ON: Strike the first (lower) note with one finger, then sound the higher note (on the same string) with another finger by fretting it without picking.

PULL-OFF: Place both fingers on the notes to be sounded. Strike the first note and without picking, pull the finger off to sound the second (lower) note.

LEGATO SLIDE: Strike the first note and then slide the same fret-hand finger up or down to the second note. The second note is not struck.

SHIFT SLIDE: Same as legato slide, except the second note is struck.

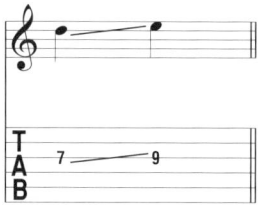

TRILL: Very rapidly alternate between the notes indicated by continuously hammering on and pulling off.

TAPPING: Hammer ("tap") the fret indicated with the pick-hand index or middle finger and pull off to the note fretted by the fret hand.

NATURAL HARMONIC: Strike the note while the fret-hand lightly touches the string directly over the fret indicated.

PINCH HARMONIC: The note is fretted normally and a harmonic is produced by adding the edge of the thumb or the tip of the index finger of the pick hand to the normal pick attack.

HARP HARMONIC: The note is fretted normally and a harmonic is produced by gently resting the pick hand's index finger directly above the indicated fret (in parentheses) while the pick hand's thumb or pick assists by plucking the appropriate string.

PICK SCRAPE: The edge of the pick is rubbed down (or up) the string, producing a scratchy sound.

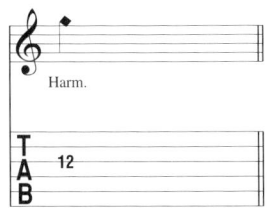 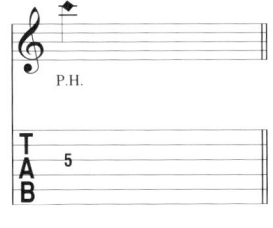 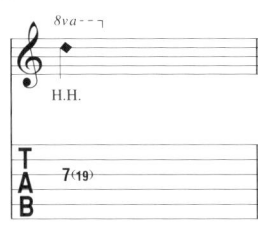 

MUFFLED STRINGS: A percussive sound is produced by laying the fret hand across the string(s) without depressing, and striking them with the pick hand.

PALM MUTING: The note is partially muted by the pick hand lightly touching the string(s) just before the bridge.

RAKE: Drag the pick across the strings indicated with a single motion.

TREMOLO PICKING: The note is picked as rapidly and continuously as possible.

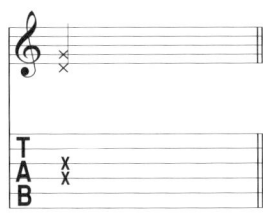 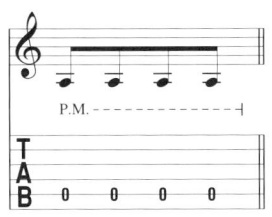  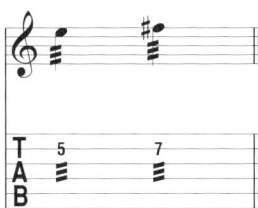

ARPEGGIATE: Play the notes of the chord indicated by quickly rolling them from bottom to top.

VIBRATO BAR DIVE AND RETURN: The pitch of the note or chord is dropped a specified number of steps (in rhythm), then returned to the original pitch.

VIBRATO BAR SCOOP: Depress the bar just before striking the note, then quickly release the bar.

VIBRATO BAR DIP: Strike the note and then immediately drop a specified number of steps, then release back to the original pitch.

 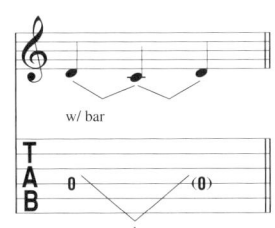 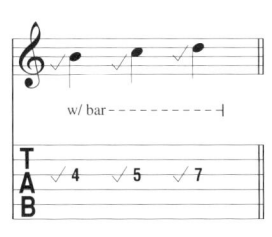 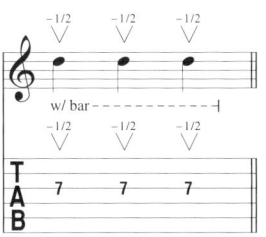

Additional Musical Definitions

(accent)	• Accentuate note (play it louder).	
(accent)	• Accentuate note with great intensity.	
(staccato)	• Play the note short.	
∎	• Downstroke	
V	• Upstroke	
D.S. al Coda	• Go back to the sign (𝄋), then play until the measure marked "*To Coda*," then skip to the section labelled "**Coda**."	
D.C. al Fine	• Go back to the beginning of the song and play until the measure marked "*Fine*" (end).	

Rhy. Fig.	• Label used to recall a recurring accompaniment pattern (usually chordal).
Riff	• Label used to recall composed, melodic lines (usually single notes) which recur.
Fill	• Label used to identify a brief melodic figure which is to be inserted into the arrangement.
Rhy. Fill	• A chordal version of a Fill.
tacet	• Instrument is silent (drops out).
	• Repeat measures between signs.
	• When a repeated section has different endings, play the first ending only the first time and the second ending only the second time.

NOTE: Tablature numbers in parentheses mean:
1. The note is being sustained over a system (note in standard notation is tied), or
2. The note is sustained, but a new articulation (such as a hammer-on, pull-off, slide or vibrato) begins, or
3. The note is a barely audible "ghost" note (note in standard notation is also in parentheses).

HOT LICKS

For the first time, the legendary Hot Licks guitar instruction video series is being made available in book format with online access to the classic video footage. All of the guitar tab from the original video booklets has been re-transcribed and edited using modern-day technology to provide you with the most accurate transcriptions ever created for this series. Plus, we've included tab for examples that were previously not transcribed, providing you with the most comprehensive Hot Licks guitar lessons yet.

The Legendary Guitar of Jason Becker	14048279
George Benson – The Art of Jazz Guitar	14048278
James Burton – The Legendary Guitar	00269774
Danny Gatton – Telemaster!	00298371
Marty Friedman – Exotic Metal Guitar	00322514
Buddy Guy – Teachin' the Blues	00253934
Warren Haynes – Electric Blues & Slide Guitar	00261616
Johnny Hiland – Chicken Pickin' Guitar	00289980
Eric Johnson – Total Electric Guitar	14048277
Brent Mason – Nashville Chops & Western Swing Guitar	14047858
Emily Remler – Bebop & Swing Guitar	00322774
Duke Robillard – Uptown Blues, Jazz Rock & Swing Guitar	00289942
The Guitar of Brian Setzer	00269775

Prices, contents, and availability subject to change without notice.

   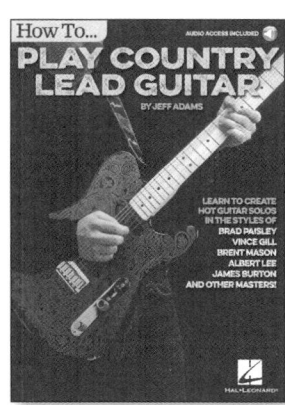 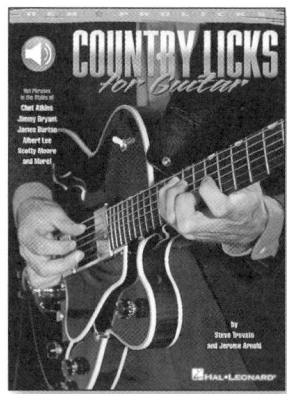

Guitar Instruction
Country Style!
from Hal Leonard

CHICKEN PICKIN' • *by Eric Halbig*

This book provides a "bird's-eye-view" of the techniques and licks common to playing hot, country lead guitar! Covers over 100 hot country guitar licks: open-string licks, double-stop licks, scales, string bending, repetitive sequences, and chromatic licks. The online audio includes 99 demonstration tracks with each lick performed at two tempos.
00695599 Book/Online Audio..................$17.99

DANIEL DONATO – THE NEW MASTER OF THE TELECASTER
PATHWAYS TO DYNAMIC SOLOS

This exclusive instructional book and DVD set includes guitar lessons taught by young Nashville phenom Daniel Donato. The "New Master of the Telecaster" shows you his unique "pathways" concept, opening your mind and fingers to uninhibited fretboard freedom, increased music theory comprehension, and more dynamic solos! The DVD features Daniel Donato himself providing full-band performances and a full hour of guitar lessons, The book includes guitar tab for all the DVD lessons and performances. Topics covered include: using chromatic notes • application of bends • double stops • analyzing different styles • and more. DVD running time: 1 hr., 4 min.
00121923 Book/DVD Pack..................$19.99

FRETBOARD ROADMAPS – COUNTRY GUITAR
The Essential Patterns That All the Pros Know and Use • *by Fred Sokolow*

This book/CD pack will teach you how to play lead and rhythm in the country style anywhere on the fretboard in any key. You'll play basic country progressions, boogie licks, steel licks, and other melodies and licks. You'll also learn a variety of lead guitar styles using moveable scale patterns, sliding scale patterns, chord-based licks, double-note licks, and more. The book features easy-to-follow diagrams and instructions for beginning, intermediate, and advanced players.
00695353 Book/CD Pack..................$16.99

HOW TO PLAY COUNTRY LEAD GUITAR
by Jeff Adams

Here is a comprehensive stylistic breakdown of country guitar techniques from the past 50 years. Drawing inspiration from the timelessly innovative licks of Merle Travis, Chet Atkins, Albert Lee, Vince Gill, Brent Mason and Brad Paisley, the near 90 musical examples within these pages will hone your left and right hands with technical string-bending and rolling licks while sharpening your knowledge of the thought process behind creating your own licks, and why and when to play them.
00131103 Book/Online Audio..................$19.99

COUNTRY LICKS FOR GUITAR
by Steve Trovato and Jerome Arnold

This unique package examines the lead guitar licks of the masters of country guitar, such as Chet Atkins, Jimmy Bryant, James Burton, Albert Lee, Scotty Moore, and many others! The online audio includes demonstrations of each lick at normal and slow speeds. The instruction covers single-string licks, pedal-steel licks, open-string licks, chord licks, rockabilly licks, funky country licks, tips on fingerings, phrasing, technique, theory, and application.
00695577 Book/Online Audo..................$19.99

COUNTRY SOLOS FOR GUITAR
by Steve Trovato

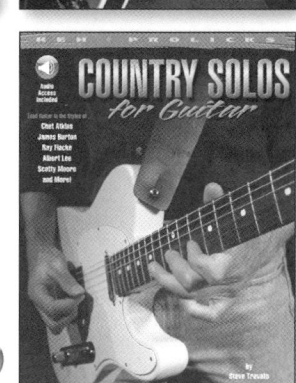

This unique book/audio pack lets guitarists examine the solo styles of axe masters such as Chet Atkins, James Burton, Ray Flacke, Albert Lee, Scotty Moore, Roy Nichols, Jerry Reed and others. It covers techniques including hot banjo rolls, funky double stops, pedal-steel licks, open-string licks and more, in standard notation and tab with phrase-by-phrase performance notes. The online audio includes full demonstrations and rhythm-only tracks.
00695448 Book/Online Audio..................$19.99

RED-HOT COUNTRY GUITAR
by Michael Hawley

The complete guide to playing lead guitar in the styles of Pete Anderson, Danny Gatton, Albert Lee, Brent Mason, and more. Includes loads of red-hot licks, techniques, solos, theory and more.
00695831 Book/Online Audio..................$19.99

25 GREAT COUNTRY GUITAR SOLOS
by Dave Rubin

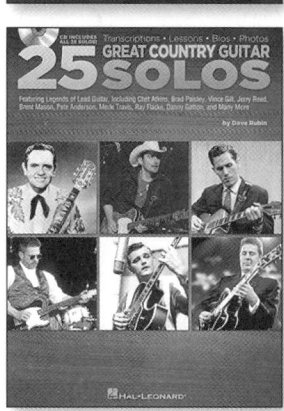

Provides solo transcriptions in notes & tab, lessons on how to play them, guitarist bios, equipment notes, photos, history, and much more. The CD contains full-band demos of every solo in the book. Songs include: Country Boy • Foggy Mountain Special • Folsom Prison Blues • Hellecaster Theme • Hello Mary Lou • I've Got a Tiger by the Tail • The Only Daddy That Will Walk the Line • Please, Please Baby • Sugarfoot Rag • and more.
00699926 Book/CD Pack..................$19.99

HAL•LEONARD®

www.halleonard.com
Prices, contents, and availability subject to change without notice.

Presenting the Best in BLUEGRASS

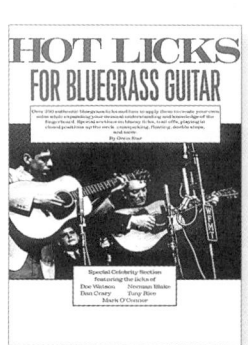

THE REAL BLUEGRASS BOOK
Ballad of Jed Clampett • Bill Cheatham • Down to the River to Pray • Foggy Mountain Top • I'm Goin' Back to Old Kentucky • John Henry • Old Train • Pretty Polly • Rocky Top • Sally Goodin • Wildwood Flower • and more.
00310910 C Instruments..............................$39.99

BLUEGRASS
Guitar Play-Along
Book/CD Pack
8 songs: Duelin' Banjos • Foggy Mountain Breakdown • Gold Rush • I Am a Man of Constant Sorrow • Nine Pound Hammer • Orange Blossom Special • Rocky Top • Wildwood Flower.
00699910 Guitar..$17.99

BLUEGRASS GUITAR
by Happy Traum
Book/CD Pack
This guitar workbook covers every aspect of bluegrass playing, from simple accompaniment to advanced instrumentals.
14004656 Guitar..$27.99

BLUEGRASS GUITAR CLASSICS
22 Carter-style solos: Back Up and Push • The Big Rock Candy Mountain • Cotton Eyed Joe • Cumberland Gap • Down Yonder • Jesse James • John Henry • Little Sadie Long Journey Home • Man of Constant Sorrow • Midnight Special • Mule Skinner Blues • Red Wing • Uncle Joe • The Wabash Cannon Ball • Wildwood Flower • and more.
00699529 Solo Guitar....................................$8.99

BLUEGRASS GUITAR
Arranged and Performed by Wayne Henderson
Transcribed by David Ziegele
Book/CD Pack
10 classic bluegrass tunes: Black Mountain Rag • Fisher's Hornpipe • Leather Britches • Lime Rock • Sally Anne • Take Me Out to the Ball Game • Temperence Reel • Twinkle Little Star • and more.
00700184 Guitar Solo..................................$16.99

BLUEGRASS SONGS FOR EASY GUITAR
25 bluegrass standards: Alabama Jubilee • Arkansas Traveler • Bill Cheatham • Blackberry Blossom • The Fox • Great Speckled Bird • I Am a Pilgrim • New River Train • Red Rocking Chair • Red Wing • Sally Goodin • Soldier's Joy • Turkey in the Straw • and more.
00702394 Easy Guitar with Notes & Tab.......$15.99

BLUEGRASS STANDARDS
by David Hamburger
16 bluegrass classics expertly arranged: Ballad of Jed Clampett • Blue Yodel No. 4 (California Blues) • Can't You Hear Me Calling • I'll Go Stepping Too • I'm Goin' Back to Old Kentucky • Let Me Love You One More Time • My Rose of Old Kentucky • We'll Meet Again Sweetheart • and more.
00699760 Solo Guitar....................................$7.99

FIRST 50 BLUEGRASS SOLOS YOU SHOULD PLAY ON GUITAR
arr. Fred Sokolow
Songs include: Arkansas Traveler • Cripple Creek • I Am a Man of Constant Sorrow • I'll Fly Away • Long Journey Home • Molly and Tenbrooks • Old Joe Clark • The Red Haired Boy • Rocky Top • Wabash Cannonball • Wayfaring Stranger • You Don't Know My Mind • and more!
00298574 Solo Guitar..................................$15.99

FRETBOARD ROADMAPS – BLUEGRASS AND FOLK GUITAR
by Fred Sokolow
Book/CD Pack
This book/CD pack will have you playing lead and rhythm anywhere on the fretboard, in any key. You'll learn chord-based licks, moveable major and blues scales, major pentatonic "sliding scales," first-position major scales, and moveable-position major scales.
00695355 Guitar..$14.99

THE GUITAR PICKER'S FAKEBOOK
by David Brody
Compiled, edited and arranged by David Brody, this is the ultimate sourcebook for the traditional guitar player. It contains over 280 jigs, reels, rags, hornpipes and breakdowns from all the major traditional instrumental styles.
14013518 Melody/Lyrics/Chords..................$32.99

O BROTHER, WHERE ART THOU?
Songs include: Big Rock Candy Mountain (Harry McClintock) • You Are My Sunshine (Norman Blake) • Hard Time Killing Floor Blues (Chris Thomas King) • I Am a Man of Constant Sorrow (The Soggy Bottom Boys/Norman Blake) • Keep on the Sunny Side (The Whites) • I'll Fly Away (Alison Krauss and Gillian Welch) • and more.
00313182 Guitar..$22.99

HOT LICKS FOR BLUEGRASS GUITAR
by Orrin Star
Over 350 authentic bluegrass licks are included in this book, which also discusses how to apply the licks to create your own solos and expand your musical understanding and knowledge of the fingerboard.
14015430 Guitar Licks..................................$26.99

www.halleonard.com

Prices, contents, and availability subject to change.